This book is dedicated to my remarkable and beloved father and first teacher, Sid Tuchman. If all fathers were as extraordinary as he, the world would be a better place.

THE FUNDAMENTALS OF (re)DESIGNING WRITING UNITS

KATHY TUCHMAN GLASS

Solution Tree | Press

a division of Solution Tree

555 North Morton Street
Bloomington, IN 47404
800.733.6786 (toll free) / 812.336.7700
FAX: 812.336.7790

email: info@SolutionTree.com
SolutionTree.com

Visit **go.SolutionTree.com/literacy** to download the free reproducibles in this book.

Printed in the United States of America

Library of Congress Control Number: 2016951882
ISBN: 978-1-942496-76-2 (paperback)

Solution Tree
Jeffrey C. Jones, CEO
Edmund M. Ackerman, President

Solution Tree Press
President: Douglas M. Rife
Editorial Director: Tonya Maddox Cupp
Managing Production Editor: Caroline Weiss
Production Editor: Alissa Voss
Senior Editor: Amy Rubenstein
Copy Chief: Sarah Payne-Mills
Proofreader: Jessi Finn
Text and Cover Designer: Abigail Bowen
Editorial Assistants: Jessi Finn and Kendra Slayton

Acknowledgments

Writing a book is an enormous undertaking. Although I have a well-defined vision of what I want to impart, articulating it clearly and concisely and organizing it well inevitably prove challenging at certain times during the writing process. I've welcomed input from others who have played vital roles at pivotal points and graciously lent their talents and input. Within my sphere of supporters, I have many to thank.

This book would not have come to fruition if it weren't for the dedication of the staff at Solution Tree. I'm grateful to those who worked behind the scenes whom I've not met in addition to those whom I recognize here.

Douglas Rife, a longtime friend and colleague, always offers prudent advice, caring support, and lively conversations. I am glad he invited me to hop on board so we can work together again and am grateful that he championed what I envisioned for this project.

Claudia Wheatley, an instantaneous friend from the get-go, helped shape the proposal until it was just right. She listened, researched, provided suggestions, and weaved her magic to ensure it was ready for prime time. I'm especially grateful to both Douglas and Claudia for helping secure our alliance for a long time to come.

Amy Rubenstein helped me as I stepped out of the gate, providing nascent feedback to launch the project in the right direction. She invited Tonya Cupp early in the process to offer necessary insight and to do what was in the best interest of my project. I appreciate their judgments and salient feedback about direction at the early stages to launch this endeavor properly.

Thanks to Rian Anderson and his team for being receptive to my suggestions and producing an eye-catching cover that beautifully integrates with the text design and visuals.

Alissa Voss, the consummate revisionary, crawled inside my head and walked around studying each room and its furnishings. She helped me sort out tough parts and rearrange others. The revision stage of the writing process should be named after her since she substantially contributed to the manuscript. Without her handiwork, it might have been a tidy mess still seeking refinement.

Technology is a vast new domain still with so much to explore. I'm grateful to Nancy Akhavan and Keli Kinsella for helping me find ways to explain the complicated world of technology in a coherent fashion so educators can access and extend their offerings to students.

I'm always indebted to Johnna Becker and Nancy Rhodes, my dear friends and go-to girls from way back when I first started my consulting career. I admire their continual willingness to maximize their own potential so they can pass on the very best in curriculum and instruction to their students.

No matter how immersed in a project Nicole Vagle is, she always lifts her head with a smile to offer feedback. She helps me tease out confusing parts that seemed clear yesterday but somehow not so much the following day. Offering valuable insight, she sets me in a new and wonderful direction that supplies me with more information to share than I thought I had in me.

Lynn Erickson has been an inspiration to me and undoubtedly countless others. Her work challenges my thinking, and her professional advice has helped to fuel a whole new venture.

For my health and well-being, I have Matt to thank. He listens to me fret about another deadline, keeps me on track, finds time in his schedule to train my weary body, and makes me smile.

The proverbial last but not least, I owe a debt of gratitude to my family. With my children graduating college and gainfully employed, my heart is full of pride and my attention clear to focus on this book. My husband, Mike, is forever my lead champion and constant advocate, always proud and understanding of the path I've chosen. His steadfast encouragement, backing, and confidence spur me on each and every day.

Visit **go.SolutionTree.com/literacy** to download the free reproducibles in this book.

Table of Contents

About the Author

Kathy Tuchman Glass is a consultant, accomplished author, and former classroom teacher with more than twenty-five years of experience in education. She provides professional development services to K–12 educators with a focus on the areas of curriculum and instruction.

Kathy is recognized for her expertise in differentiated instruction, standards work around English language arts, literacy, instructional strategies, teaching methods, and backward planning for unit and lesson design. She is a member of the International Literacy Association, the National Council of Teachers of English, the Association for Supervision and Curriculum Development, and Learning Forward.

She earned a bachelor's degree from Indiana University–Bloomington and a master's degree in education from San Francisco State University.

To learn more about Kathy's work, visit www.kathyglassconsulting.com.

To book Kathy Tuchman Glass for professional development, contact pd@SolutionTree.com.

Introduction

Writing is an integral part of students' education. It is not just about the art of communicating and expressing oneself well for different audiences and purposes; writing also expands and embeds learning (Graham & Hebert, 2010). When we write about what we read, we grasp the content more fully. It is a powerful and effective means for learning in every subject area, and the possibilities for written discourse across disciplines are endless. For example, in social studies, students write historical journal entries from the point of view of an individual experiencing a past event; in science, students take detailed observational lab notes; in mathematics, students justify their solutions to a mathematics problem; and in physical education, students record the rules and instructions for how to play a game. Writing is a 21st century skill, and the benefits of learning to write well have far-reaching implications, as stated in *Writing Next* (Graham & Perin, 2007), a report commissioned by the Carnegie Corporation of New York that discusses research-based techniques to improve writing:

> Young people who do not have the ability to transform thoughts, experiences, and ideas into written words are in danger of losing touch with the joy of inquiry, the sense of intellectual curiosity, and the inestimable satisfaction of acquiring wisdom that are the touchstones of humanity. (p. 1)

What to Expect

What you hold in your hands is a foundational book that explains and provides examples of the fundamentals of unit and lesson design for teaching writing. The text will guide you in designing or redesigning and conducting a smooth, well-integrated unit of instruction for writing that raises the bar for students and builds your professional capacity. To this end, it will broadly discuss four specific writing *types* (also called *categories* or *modes*)—(1) narrative, (2) descriptive, (3) persuasive, and (4) expository—and their related genres. This book's chief aim is to spell out the components and steps of a backward planning approach for unit design and provide templates, tools, methods, examples, and strategies to help you plan a quality unit with lessons that will guide and empower students to produce a sound written product. My ultimate goal is to help you develop curriculum and deliver instruction with depth, rigor, and clarity.

What you'll receive from this book are the guidance, tools, and wherewithal to be judicious and intentional about the following.

- **Designing new units:** Some educators may read this book and develop a writing unit from scratch. The unit can focus on writing in an English language arts class (such as a realistic fiction short story or literary critique), in a content area (such as an informational report about a topic in science or history), or for an interdisciplinary unit that culminates in a writing project.
- **Redesigning existing units:** Others may redesign an existing unit. This includes revising all or part of a unit you previously wrote or have at your disposal, such as one a colleague passed on to you, a unit you found online, or curriculum from a publisher. Reasons for redesigning a unit might be that the culminating assessment isn't rigorous enough, it needs more engaging activities, or it requires better guiding questions.
- **Critiquing adopted textbook materials or curriculum:** Still other readers may evaluate published material to ensure it meets rigorous standards. Some resources might include

> an overwhelming amount of effective (and ineffective) strategies, activities, assessments, pedagogy, writing ideas, and so forth. With fresh eyes, you'll learn to critique what is available and make conscientious decisions about what to include for your students, such as bypassing mediocre material or using or revising what's provided to conduct an effective, engaging writing unit that improves student learning and output.

This book is primarily for teachers, curriculum designers, and literacy coaches who support students in grades 5–12. If you also work with elementary students, you can adapt the material as needed. You can read this book and work independently on your unit or read it with colleagues and plan a writing unit together as a department, interdisciplinary team, professional book club, or a collaborative team working within the context of a professional learning community. In whatever configuration you choose to work, consider how teachers across subject areas can assume responsibility for teaching skills that contribute to strong written products. Working as a team allows teachers to delineate expectations so all writing skills are addressed and not left as assumptions that are inadvertently missed.

Singleton teachers (teachers who are the only ones in their school responsible for teaching a particular grade level or subject) can collaborate with job-alike colleagues to brainstorm and create a unit together. Logistically, they might create a Google Doc (or use another electronic collaborative tool) so each can contribute to the pieces that will eventually make for the final product of a robust writing unit. If you teach in a small district without the benefit of subject-area colleagues, consider working virtually with others in the same position in other counties or schools. Alternatively, you can collaborate with content-area teachers in or across appropriate grade clusters in your school. For any collegial situation, or if working with others is not feasible, this book provides tools to re-envision what and how to teach writing to students.

What This Book Is Not

Although this book will prepare students for writing situations in standardized tests, it is not about helping students respond to an on-demand writing prompt in a timed situation. You might, however, issue such a prompt for pre- or formative assessments within your writing unit to inform instruction. My focus in this book is about redesigning or designing a complete and rigorous writing unit in which students advance through the steps of the writing process. As such, use analytic rubrics to score and as an instructional tool to gather information to improve the quality of writing. Know, however, that when students participate in a demanding and engaging writing unit, it prepares them well for a district- or state-mandated test:

> In schools with a major emphasis on standardized tests, teachers are prone to conclude that their own assessments must always approximate the nature of the year-end standardized test so students will be "ready" for that test when it comes. . . . However, we ought not to lose sight of the fact that if all teaching is proscribed by the very limited and limiting format of a particular test, students' learning experiences are woefully restricted. . . . If they learn better because of how we teach and assess them, it's likely they will fare better on standardized tests than if we insist on teaching them in narrow ways that are ineffective for them. When learning "works" for a student, that student is likely to enter a testing situation both more competently and confidently than would otherwise have been the case, and outcomes should be predictably better. Further, the student is more likely to find learning itself a positive experience and one worth repeating rather than avoiding. (Tomlinson & Moon, 2013, p. 46)

Therefore, it behooves you to avoid aligning every task to a standardized test–like prompt or situation. Rather, this book will help you teach writing effectively across a range of text types and genres and supplant the necessary skills to embolden students to approach any writing situation with courage and assurance.

Book Overview

The Fundamentals of (Re)designing Writing Units is predicated on sound pedagogy and serves to foreground your understanding of unit design with an emphasis on crafting units around writing types and genres. It will also provide recommendations and strategies for writing in general and is necessary reading in order to effectively create units for specific genres you will target, such as argumentation essays, realistic fiction, autobiographies, or informational reports. This book has an accompanying online landing page with free downloadable materials—templates, checklists, rubrics, assessments, writing prompts, and more—to support unit design and lesson implementation. Visit **go.SolutionTree.com/literacy** to download the free reproducibles in this book.

Chapter 1 summarizes the research related to writing and provides recommendations for instruction, including explicitly teaching the steps to the writing process, identifying clear expectations for a writing task, summarizing, and other suggestions. It also presents an overview of the different writing types, their characteristics and purposes, and the many associated genres that fall under each.

Chapter 2 focuses on the six stages of the writing process and various instructional strategies: (1) prewriting, (2) drafting, (3) revising (through self-assessing and receiving feedback), (4) editing, (5) publishing, and (6) reflecting. You'll also read about digital communities and technological resources students can use throughout the writing process.

Chapter 3 tackles the backward planning approach to unit design. I highlight the beginning stage of this approach—identifying standards and using them to articulate what you want students to know (K), understand (U), and be able to do (D)—and provide examples of unit- and lesson-guiding questions.

Chapter 4 continues the backward planning approach by focusing on evidence of student learning, particularly culminating writing assessments. I feature types of performance assessments, ways to craft writing prompts and examples, the benefits of student writing checklists, and a discussion about types of rubrics—analytic and holistic—to assess writing with an emphasis on the former. Additionally, I touch on the importance of using checklists, rubrics, and student writing models as key instructional tools. Suggestions for grading, calibrating papers, and finding anchor papers so there is consistency in scoring among colleagues are also presented. This chapter concludes with preassessment ideas for writing.

Chapter 5 moves to lesson design, specifically using gradual release of responsibility as a model for teaching new learning (such as skill, strategy, or process). I explain each phase of this lesson approach along with a concrete lesson example you can use in your classroom. Additionally, I provide several ideas for differentiating instruction.

Chapter 6 is all about launching the unit. The text describes piloting the unit and reflecting on lessons to perfect the design and provides revision suggestions for the next time you teach this unit.

Finally, the appendices provide a complete list of all figures and tables included in the book for easy reference. They also offer professional and student resources, such as links to general writing resources, rubrics, student writing models, sources for complex text, essay contests and submissions, and more.

By the end of reading, you will be fully versed in all the fundamental steps of writing unit design and have the tools to implement this rewarding work in your classroom.

CHAPTER

1

Writing Instruction Recommendations and an Introduction to Writing Types

We take for granted the fact that writing must be taught in school. After all, it's part of the age-old trifecta of Rs: reading, writing, and arithmetic. In truth, there are logical reasons and benefits to mastering the art of written discourse, as mentioned in the introduction to this book and in this chapter. Plus, there are proven methods educators can employ to teach students this craft. Since our youth are unfortunately underperforming, learning to write proficiently is an imperative that needs critical attention. I'll address these points at the beginning of this chapter with specific emphasis on research findings and instructional practice recommendations gleaned from two reports—*Writing Next: Effective Strategies to Improve Writing of Adolescents in Middle and High Schools* (Graham & Perin, 2007) and *Writing to Read: Evidence for How Writing Can Improve Reading* (Graham & Hebert, 2010). The latter document, which emphasizes the impact writing can have on reading comprehension, builds on the findings of the former report. Later in the chapter, I'll delineate different types of writing and their associated genres and subgenres to give you an overview of the realm of writing opportunities for teaching and learning.

Writing Next authors Steve Graham and Dolores Perin (2007) state a compelling case for the imperative to increase adolescents' writing abilities:

> Writing well is not just an option for young people—it is a necessity. Along with reading comprehension, writing skill is a predictor of academic success and a basic requirement for participation in civic life and in the global economy. Yet every year in the United States large numbers of adolescents graduate from high school unable to write at the basic levels required by colleges or employers. (p. 3)

These authors cite disconcerting findings, among them the stagnation of adolescent literacy levels and that 70 percent of fourth- to twelfth-grade students are low-achieving writers (Graham & Perin, 2007). A study from the College Board, a panel established by the National Commission on Writing (2005), reports the troubling statistic that U.S. businesses spend an estimated $3.1 billion each year on remedial writing training. Furthermore, a collaborative effort of four organizations, including the Partnership for 21st Century Skills, gathered responses from more than four hundred U.S. employers in 2006. Among other survey results, they indicate writing as the weakest area: "Employer respondents report 'deficiencies' in *Writing in English*, *Mathematics*, and *Reading Comprehension*, skills considered 'important' for successful job performance. At the top, with nearly three-quarters of employer respondents (72.0 percent) rating high school graduates as 'deficient,' is *Writing in English*" (Casner-Lotto & Barrington, 2006, p. 34). However, there are actions educators can take to turn this cycle around and help students reach their potential as writers and glean the benefits.

Writing Instruction Recommendations

With this call to arms, Graham and Perin (2007) collected, reviewed, and analyzed 136 experimental and quasi-experimental studies on adolescent writing. Through the statistical method of meta-analysis, they could "determine the *consistency* and *strength* of the effects of instructional practices on student writing quality and . . . highlight those practices that hold the most promise" (p. 4). The results of their work yielded eleven recommendations of research-proven instructional methods to improve writing skills for students in grades 4–12 (see Elements of Effective Adolescent Writing Instruction on page 6). Note that the authors admit that more research is needed to highlight what works well to improve students' writing abilities and to consider new target areas. To this point, since writing instruction encompasses a wide range of complex skills, other practices besides those in their list deserve attention so students receive the best advantage of premium instruction.

Elements of Effective Adolescent Writing Instruction

Following is a list of elements of effective adolescent writing instruction as Graham and Perin (2007) outline.

- **Writing strategies:** Explicitly and methodically teach each step of the writing process (prewriting, drafting, revising, editing, publishing, and reflecting) with the intent that students eventually incorporate the steps independently. (These steps are discussed in more detail in chapter 2.)
- **Summarization:** Identify the structure and characteristics of a summary and systematically teach how to produce summaries of a text.
- **Collaborative writing:** Orchestrate situations during stages of the writing process in which students work collaboratively—for instance, to brainstorm ideas together, share and discuss research, and give each other feedback on drafts.
- **Specific product goals:** Articulate reachable expectations specific to a writing task, including the purpose for and characteristics of the writing. Identify the overarching goal, such as producing an argument, and set discrete objectives along the way that contribute to the whole (such as staking a claim, identifying logical reasons, and researching to determine supporting evidence).
- **Word processing:** Make electronic devices available to produce written work, and show how the devices can be useful instructional supports (such as to add, delete, and move text or to collaborate with others via technology to exchange feedback).
- **Sentence combining:** Teach how to craft more complex and sophisticated sentences to enhance the quality of writing.
- **Prewriting:** Create instructional experiences to help students generate and organize ideas prior to composing a first draft for a specific writing task.
- **Inquiry activities:** Provide opportunities for students to read, collect, and analyze data (observations, comparison and contrast of case studies, researched evidence) before they write to help them develop ideas and content for a particular writing task.
- **Process writing approach:** Conduct a comprehensive writing unit composed of a series of lessons or workshops that each target interwoven skills necessary to produce a sound written piece, allow uninterrupted writing time as well as collaboration, address authentic audiences, differentiate learning to meet individual needs, and embed instruction on the steps of the writing process.
- **Study models:** Use writing models as an instructional tool for students to analyze and emulate a particular writing genre.

- **Writing for content learning:** Use writing as a vehicle to learn content material.

Steve Graham and Michael Hebert (2010), in their publication *Writing to Read*, affirm the interconnected benefits of reading and writing. They assert that writing has the potential to improve students' reading in three ways:

> First, reading and writing are both functional activities that can be combined to accomplish specific goals, such as learning new ideas presented in a text (Fitzgerald & Shanahan, 2000). For instance, writing about information in a science text should facilitate comprehension and learning, as it provides the reader with a means for recording, connecting, analyzing, personalizing, and manipulating key ideas from the text. Second, reading and writing are connected, as they draw upon common knowledge and cognitive processes (Shanahan, 2006). Consequently, improving students' writing skills should result in improved reading skills. Third, reading and writing are both communication activities, and writers should gain insight about reading by creating their own texts (Tierney & Shanahan, 1991), leading to better comprehension of texts produced by others. (p. 4)

When students write about what they read, teachers can discover if there are any misconceptions that need addressing or if students are on target with content acquisition. They can clarify, question, and reflect on the material through writing to make sense of it and extend their thinking, which contributes to retention, as well.

Strengthening Reading Through Writing

Along with the previous list from *Writing Next*, consider the following effective practices from Graham and Hebert (2010) to help guide your curriculum planning.

- **Write about the text:** To grasp the content students read across disciplines, devise tasks in which they analyze, interpret, and provide insight by writing summaries, notes, responses to questions, and questions and answers about the text. Note that the research reveals that although answers can be offered verbally, recording written answers helps students remember them better; plus, this practice allows them to review and reevaluate them later (Emig, 1977, as cited in Graham & Hebert, 2010). When students write for different purposes about the content they read, they continuously return to the text, each time deepening their understanding and knowledge base as they verify, reflect, summarize, connect key ideas within and across texts, and more.
- **Teach writing skills and processes:** Since both reading and writing share common processes and knowledge, it behooves educators to teach writing since it has a correlation to reading comprehension success. Specifically, instruct students how to construct and combine sentences, build and structure paragraphs and longer texts, and identify common characteristics among writing types and genres.
- **Ask students to write frequently:** Instructing students to write in a variety of ways across subject areas in and outside of school can promote their comprehension. Arrange for students to select their own topics, determine topics with peers, or assign writing so they have consistent practice, such as writing letters to pen pals, journal entries, or responses to quick writes.

The recommended practices from *Writing to Read* and *Writing Next* can enhance, support, and ground the teaching of writing. Although the recommendations are based on careful research, the authors are clear to point out that they do not represent an entire curriculum. Rather, educators can use the recommendations as guidance for developing a robust writing program and will likely combine two or more suggestions during a learning experience. For example, you might define and explain the compound-complex sentence type, share published samples of text that utilize this sentence construction, and model how to combine sentences to produce it. Then ask students to collaborate with peers to write a paragraph with various sentence types, including compound-complex sentences.

Lessons and activities within this book emanate from these recommendations and others and represent worthwhile and effective writing practices. As mentioned in Graham and Perin's (2007) list, an effective writing unit supports a *process approach*—composed of lessons or workshops targeting interwoven skills that ultimately culminate in a complete and developed writing product. This book highlights the writing process along with other recommendations that can work in concert to improve students' writing capabilities. When beginning creation of a writing unit, though, it is important to understand the purpose behind the writing, which will lend itself to identifying a particular type of text and genre.

Writing Types and Genres

Genre is a term used across artistic work: writing genres, musical genres, and film genres. When different works share commonalities—like a distinctive style, form, or element—they are grouped together in a genre. For example, country music is a genre typically characterized by string instruments (like a fiddle, banjo, or guitar), the lyrics tend to be about problems people encounter, and artists and their followers hail largely from the South or Midwest. Some genres are divided even further by subgenres; country music, for instance, can include honky-tonk, bluegrass, folk, country pop, and so forth.

Genres reside under writing *types*, which are also called modes, categories, or styles. However, there is currently no consensus on how many writing types exist or what their names are. The Common Core identifies three text types: (1) argumentation, (2) informational and explanatory, and (3) narrative. States that do not use the Common Core, as well as provinces, might adhere to other classifications in their standards documents; for example, Virginia specifies these long-standing categories: (1) narration, (2) exposition, (3) description, and (4) persuasion. Similarly, for the purpose of this book, I will be identifying four writing types—(1) narrative, (2) descriptive, (3) expository, and (4) persuasive—and focusing on the genres within these types.

Each text type is aligned to a writer's purpose for crafting the piece, which in turn dictates other writing factors like audience and style. If writing to inform or explain, a writer will create an expository piece like a technical manual or article. If the purpose is to entertain, the writer will compose a narrative, such as a mystery or fantasy novel. Refer to table 1.1 to see these categorizations along with their characteristics, primary purposes, and specific genres. Although the table is comprehensive, feel free to adapt it to add other genres or subgenres to the list.

Since there are alternate ways to name each overarching text type and the many genres and subgenres within them, your list for extensive digital or print searches may yield somewhat different, yet complementary, information. Therefore, my advice is to be consistent across your school and district so that you, your colleagues, and your students are using similar terminology and explanations and are addressing the necessary standards linked to particular text types or genres. In this book, I use the terminology reflected in table 1.1.

Some text can distinctively fall into one type, and throughout the entire work, readers clearly recognize it along with the author's purpose for writing. However, this is not always the case. Some works blend types and genres. In fact, as indicated in table 1.1, descriptive text can be embedded throughout many genres. For example, a procedural paper, mystery, or autobiography might each include sections of description sprinkled throughout. A business letter might contain elements of persuasion. Or an infomercial might include narrative features. Furthermore, a realistic contemporary fiction piece could include aspects of informational text within it, such as a character who perhaps provides a how-to sequence of steps to accomplish a task that is part of the plot. Regardless of merging some types or genres, writers should have an overarching purpose that designates one prominent text type.

Although I've discussed prose and will continue to do so throughout the book, poetry also deserves attention, though it does not fit into the table of general writing types. Poetry—which dates back to approximately 3000 BC—uses a rhythmic structure and more aesthetic language than prose. It was recited orally in ancient times and used to record cultural history, tell stories, relay news of the day, and remember information.

During a poetry unit, students can learn to appreciate and craft various poems, which communicate language quite powerfully using fewer words than are used in prose. Poets rely on sensory, descriptive language to stir emotions, express feelings, and leave a lasting impression about an individual, topic, or idea. They base their work on connotation rather than denotation, expecting their readers to examine the deeper meanings behind their words and make inferences and interpretations to arrive at new insights. To obtain an artistic quality, features of sound, such as rhyme, rhythm, assonance, consonance,

Table 1.1: Writing Types—Characteristics, Purposes, and Genres

Writing Type	Characteristics	Primary Purposes	Genres and Subgenres

Narrative (Fiction)	• Fictional narratives are based on the imagination.
	• Fictional narratives include elements of literature: plot, character, setting, point of view, and theme.
	• Some subgenres, such as contemporary realistic and historical fiction, include facts.
	• Writers can utilize a host of literary techniques, such as suspense, foreshadowing, dialect, dialogue, allusion, and so forth, as well as descriptive details and figurative language (such as imagery and simile).
	• Plot forms the basic structure that chronicles how the events unfold naturally and in a logical order.
	  ◦ Plot elements include introduction, central conflict, rising action, climax, falling action, and resolution (denouement).
	  ◦ More sophisticated writers might include flashbacks, flash-forwards, or parallel or multiple plotlines.
	  ◦ Developing writers can create a beginning, middle, and ending or a problem and solution as a starting point for producing a plot.
		• To entertain
		• To describe
			Folktale
			• Fairy tale
			• Legend
			• Myth
			• Animal tale
			  ◦ Fable
			  ◦ Pourquoi
			  ◦ Trickster
			Fantasy
			• High and low fantasy
			• Science fiction
			• Tall tale
			Realistic fiction
			• Contemporary realistic fiction
			• Historical fiction
			• Mystery

Narrative (Nonfiction)	• Unlike fictional narrative, nonfictional narration is based on facts and is informative rather than fictitious.
	• Genres in this category can include some elements of literature but with a different treatment.
	  ◦ The characters are actual people.
	  ◦ All genres do not follow a plot structure.
	• Writers of narrative nonfiction may utilize literary techniques such as dialogue, allusion, symbolism, and irony, as well as descriptive details and figurative language (such as imagery and metaphor).
		• To inform
		• To describe
			• Autobiography
			• Biography
			• Memoir
			• Personal narrative

Descriptive	• Writers describe an object, topic, character, person, place, experience, situation, emotion, or event so readers can visualize it. • Descriptions are organized and can stand alone or be incorporated within narrative text (such as a description of a setting, character, or individual) or expository writing (such as a description of steps to perform a task or parts of a plant). • This type of writing includes precise and vivid language and relies heavily on figurative language (such as imagery, simile, or metaphor).	• To describe	• (Descriptive text is included in various genres.) • Eyewitness report • Field notes • Journal or diary writing • Nature log

continued ➤

Writing Type	Characteristics	Primary Purposes	Genres and Subgenres
Expository	• Expository text presents factual information that, depending on the genre, is sometimes based on research (for example, a research report or technical manual). • The writer informs or offers an explanation to readers about a topic through facts, definitions, details, examples, and other pertinent information. • These writing genres typically include a particular format and text features (such as a table of contents, a glossary, an index, realistic illustrations or photos, charts, diagrams, and subheadings). • The structure of exposition can vary depending on the purpose of the piece, such as comparison and contrast, problem-solution, cause and effect, chronological, or procedural. • Expository papers (essays and reports) have an introduction, including a thesis statement; well-structured body paragraphs with a topic sentence, supporting details, and an ending sentence; and a conclusion.	• To explain • To inform • To describe	• Brochure • Business letter and memorandum • Directions • Encyclopedia entry • Essay (compare and contrast, cause and effect, and so on) • Historical document • How-to or procedural document • Informational report • Instructions • Interview • Literary analysis • Magazine or newspaper article • Observational notes • Proposal • Recipes • Research report • Resume • Science lab report • Summary or précis • Technical manual
Persuasive	• Persuasive genres present a position on a particular issue or topic and use persuasive techniques to sway readers (or listeners) to the writer's point of view, to convince them to take an action, to change their behavior or beliefs, to ask them to support a policy, or to accept an explanation or evaluation. • Writers make a claim that is articulated in a clear thesis statement. Reasons and evidence support the position. • One or more of Aristotle's rhetorical appeals (ethos, logos, pathos) are included in persuasive pieces. Argumentation—a genre within this type—can include all three appeals; however, it relies heavily on logos, or logic, since writers research to find logical reasoning and relevant evidence (facts, data, examples, and so forth) culled from credible sources. • Advanced writers of arguments acknowledge and address counterarguments. • Persuasive pieces can be based more on opinion and include unsubstantiated evidence to support the claim (for example, propaganda and advertisements).	• To persuade	• Advertisement or infomercial • Argumentation essay (or speech) • Book or movie review • Commentary • Letter to the editor; editorial • Letter of recommendation • Letter of complaint • Literary critique (or literary argument) • Persuasive letter (social action letter) • Political speech or other speech • Resume cover letter

and alliteration, are characteristic of this form of communication. Additionally, poets heavily infuse devices, such as imagery, simile, metaphor, personification, apostrophe, tone, symbolism, allusion, and so forth, to achieve an intended effect. Poetry can be divided into three main groups: (1) lyric (such as odes, sonnets, and haikus), (2) narrative (for example, epics and ballads), and (3) dramatic.

Writing Continuum

It is prudent to have students read texts and produce writing that cover a wide range of genres across grade levels and subjects under the umbrella of a particular type. For example, students should have the opportunity across the grades to hone reading and writing skills related to narrative fiction, such as fairy tales, myths, historical fiction, realistic contemporary fiction, and other such text. For expository, students can write different genres across content areas, such as a lab report in science and a cause-and-effect essay in history to demonstrate understanding of factors associated with past events. With this attention within and across grades and subject areas, students will steadily and progressively develop a thorough understanding of the structure and elements of many genres. As a consequence, students can make conscientious and confident decisions about writing for a variety of purposes and audiences in and outside of school. Additionally, this learning supports *disciplinary literacy*—using reading, writing, speaking, and listening as a means to acquire and apply content knowledge, core concepts, and experiences and skills within content areas, including critical thinking and understanding how experts in a discipline utilize specialized tools and resources to accomplish their work.

To this point, you might consider spearheading or suggesting a project in which you and colleagues create a writing continuum using content standards as a guide that articulates how the school or district covers teaching genres across grades and subjects. This could be part of a curriculum-mapping project that reveals unnecessary repetition and gaps in the writing curriculum. Figure 1.1 (page 12) provides a partial sample of a format a school or district might use as a jumping-off point to map what teachers in each grade and content area have students produce. Please visit **go.SolutionTree.com/literacy** for a plethora of resources, including figure 1.1, which can be adapted to include other genres and grades K–12. To use it, ask each teacher to complete the chart. Then come together as a group to discuss individual entries. It is likely that you will have to first discuss what each genre entails before teachers complete the chart. With finished charts in hand, discuss their entries and address these and other pertinent questions.

- Are some genres repeated across grades or content areas? Are others missing?
- What genres within a text type are standards based and most important to cover? Are some genres essential to acquire learning in certain content areas?
- To what degree do teachers cover specific standards related directly to genres (myth, research report) and associated writing standards (for example, employing the writing process, conducting research based on focused questions, or gathering information from multiple sources)? Do teachers use rubrics and student checklists that reflect these expectations?
- Do students have time in and outside of class to progress through all the stages of the writing process? How much time is dedicated to each stage during class?
- Are there standards-based genres that are not taught fully but students are expected to produce this writing independently?
- What specific skills are formally taught in order to produce the written piece?

Although language arts teachers use writing standards as a cornerstone of their instruction along with other literacy standards, all subject-area teachers can expect students to produce a coherent and organized written piece. Therefore, hold conversations, commit to using writing to contribute to disciplinary knowledge, and work together across content areas to identify and teach necessary writing skills. This practice will help ensure we are aptly supporting all our students to succeed, ensure that nothing is left to chance, and support collegial collaboration to teach writing. For instance, a science teacher focuses on the structure and elements of a lab report (introduction, statement of problem, hypothesis, materials, and so forth). To support this assignment, the language arts teacher addresses sentence structure, citation conventions, and consistent, objective point of view, along with other key writing skills required to produce this report.

Writing Continuum

Teacher: ______________________ **Grade Level:** ______________________

Subject Area: ____

Directions: In each box, indicate to what degree you teach a genre:

S Input an S if you meet a standard fully and conduct a comprehensive unit around the expectations.

/ Place a forward slash in the box if you conduct some lessons around the genre.

✓ Place a check mark if you assign a genre as an in-class or homework assignment and do not formally teach the skills associated with it.

If you do not assign or teach the writing genre, leave the box empty.

	Grade							
Narrative	**5**	**6**	**7**	**8**	**9**	**10**	**11**	**12**
Fiction Genres								
Fairy tale								
Myth or legend								
Animal tale (fable, pourquoi, trickster)								
High or low fantasy								
Science fiction								
Tall tale								
Contemporary realistic fiction								
Historical fiction								
Mystery								
Nonfiction Genres								
Autobiography								
Biography								
Memoir								
Personal narrative								
Expository	**5**	**6**	**7**	**8**	**9**	**10**	**11**	**12**
Brochure								
Business letter or memo								
Directions or instructions								
Compare-and-contrast essay								
Cause-and-effect essay								
Problem-solution essay								
How-to or procedural document								
Informational or research report								
Interview								
Literary analysis								
Magazine or newspaper article								
Observational notes								
Proposal								
Resume								
Science lab report								
Summary or précis								
Technical manual								

Figure 1.1: Sample writing continuum.

Visit ***go.SolutionTree.com/literacy*** *for a free reproducible version of this figure.*

As a result of completing figure 1.1 and after collaborative discussions with colleagues, decide which genres and skills teachers in specific grades and content areas should address. Generate a new document that reflects these decisions across the district or school. Additionally, enter specific standards that will be addressed so teachers have guidance for curriculum planning.

Summary

Research shows the urgent need to improve students' writing capacity (Graham & Perin, 2007) and the advantages that are associated with strong writing skills, including improvements in reading comprehension (Graham & Hebert, 2010). Writing about what we read helps extend and reinforce learning, and both are intrinsically linked communication processes (Graham & Hebert, 2010).

When teachers design a writing unit, a host of research-based recommendations can enhance teachers' repertoire of teaching methods and instructional practice to support students' proficiency. Among the many strategies are explicitly teaching writing process steps, articulating clear expectations for a finished product, collaborating during the writing process, and sentence combining, among others (Graham & Perin, 2007). To use writing as a vehicle to promote deeper introspection of reading material, teachers can devise tasks such as writing summaries, notes, and responses. Additionally, instructing students to write frequently across subject areas is another path toward comprehension (Graham & Hebert, 2010).

Literature is divided into two forms of expression—(1) poetry and (2) prose. Prose is relatively straightforward and pragmatic in its approach. On the other hand, poetry relies on comparisons, sounds, imagery, and other techniques to evoke feelings and communicate in a deeply artistic manner. Each text type (or category or mode) for prose—narrative, descriptive, expository, and persuasive—also contains a variety of genres and even subgenres. Given proper instructional experiences about the elements, structure, and format of specific genres within each text type, students can better understand the utility and purpose of each one and successfully produce writing pieces across grades and disciplines. It would be helpful to work with colleagues to create a writing continuum that articulates which genres and specific skills subject-area teachers should address alone or in collaboration with colleagues, as appropriate.

Following this introduction to writing and writing types, chapter 2 contains a thorough discussion of the stages of the writing process. Since this book is predicated on designing a unit to teach the characteristics and structure for targeted writing genres, these steps are critical in learning how to formulate a sound, comprehensive written piece. I also discuss options for incorporating digital environments, online resources, and apps within writing units to support digital learners.

CHAPTER

2

The Stages of the Writing Process and Digital Environments

Although the writing process has evolved over time, D. Gordon Rohman (1965) is credited as the initial source of the three-stage model that comprised (1) prewriting, (2) writing, and (3) rewriting. The process is now more expansive and is often presented with the first five of the following stages. Some researchers include reflecting as an additional sixth stage, which I believe to be prudent.

1. Prewriting
2. Drafting
3. Revising
4. Editing
5. Publishing
6. Reflecting

Writing Next points to the benefits of teaching students the stages of the writing process so they can produce well-constructed products: "Teaching adolescents strategies for planning, revising, and editing their compositions has shown a dramatic effect on the quality of students' writing" (Graham & Perin, 2007, p. 15). This process is meant to be instructive. Therefore, deliberately teach each step in a systematic way so students apply what they learn directly to their own work to maximize the likelihood of achieving optimal results. Ruie Pritchard and Ronald Honeycutt (2006) explain:

> In general, those studies that view the process model as encompassing more teacher direction in the process show positive effects on the quality of students' writing, on their view of themselves as writers, and on their understanding of the writing process. (p. 276)

During unit planning, devise lessons not only about the process but also to address skills related to specific genre elements, plus the craft of writing in general that makes written discourse comprehensible. For example, teach narrative techniques of dialogue and descriptive detail, or show how to select relevant facts and definitions for an informational report. As well, teach skills related to grammar usage and conventions. To aid in lesson planning, the rest of this book provides useful tools, strategies, and resources.

Although once thought to be a series of ordered and linear steps, the writing process is widely known to be recursive as students move in and out of the stages to produce their work (Pritchard & Honeycutt, 2006). Each step is not an entity unto itself but rather overlaps with others, and movement between them is expected and even encouraged. For example, when building an argument, a writer might determine during a second draft that his argument is weak in evidence. This may suggest returning to prewriting to analyze research and gather more support. Also, writers usually revise more than once as new ideas emerge from peer or teacher input. Aside from the process being flexible, writers can customize it. In this regard, each person might take a differentiated pathway to publication, progressing through the steps in a different order and varying the time spent dedicated to each stage.

Not everything that students write needs to progress through the writing process. Sometimes there are mini-tasks that do not require all six steps. For example, you might ask students to freewrite to stimulate their thoughts on a topic related to a new unit. Or perhaps student pairs collaborate to write dialogue that they envision two characters might engage in based on their understanding of the interactions between them. However, the culminating assessment of the writing unit that you will craft as a result of reading this book calls for students to synthesize the various skills they learn to produce a well-developed written product.

This book is meant to support you in (re)designing an extensive unit that culminates in a standards-based writing piece. As mentioned, using the steps in the writing process will assist with student achievement in this kind of in-depth writing. Therefore, in this chapter, I explain each stage and provide some examples for instruction. Depending on the grade you teach and your students' experience with these steps, you may not necessarily need to explicitly teach each one. Students might already be well versed in all or some of the stages through previous years of instruction. In fact, the eventual goal is for students to become proficient writers who internalize steps in the process and implement them in an effective order for different genres, and do so independently and with automaticity (Pritchard & Honeycutt, 2006).

Although all stages are important, I dedicate considerable discussion to the revision stage, particularly feedback and suggestions for how peers, parents or guardians, and teachers can offer it, as well as self-assessment. This attention to feedback given throughout the writing process is well warranted because research credits it as a key contributor to progress and improvement: "Formative assessment, consisting of lots of feedback and opportunities to use that feedback, enhances performance and achievement" (Wiggins, 2012, p. 10).

At the end of the chapter, I provide several options to incorporate electronic tools and apps into a writing unit. In a society rife with technology, it is important to investigate technological opportunities to support learning goals and help students in their endeavors. For example, you may wish to consider ways students will collect and store their work, choose whether students will utilize online portfolios for collating and displaying work, or set up online options for students to collaborate at various points during the writing process. These suggestions and resources for how to productively and effectively utilize technology to enhance what students do at strategic points appear in the section on Using Digital Environments During the Writing Process, beginning on page 31. Since available options in this arena are ever changing, pervasive, and expanding, what I provide are starting points for you to investigate how you can use them to meet specific goals.

Prewriting

The critical step of prewriting readies writers for their first draft. It is what writers do to prepare for writing, and this detailed planning helps ensure a writing project starts on the right course. During this stage, students read the task instructions and identify the purpose and audience associated with it. Additionally, they learn the criteria via a checklist or rubric so they are fully aware of expectations. They set goals and generate ideas by performing any number of exercises to stimulate thoughts. To foster idea collection, students might participate in one or a combination of these or similar activities.

- Brainstorm items or questions.
- Complete a graphic organizer (see the list of websites in the appendix for ideas).
- Make a chart, graph, or table.
- Engage in a freewrite.
- Generate word associations.
- Take notes.
- Interview someone.
- Draw pictures or diagrams.
- Discuss ideas with peers.
- Conduct research in print and online.

Students then review what they created and make sense of their ideas. They arrange and organize them in a structure that aligns to the task and its purpose, taking into account the genre they will write. For example, a story follows a plotline, so they might take their ideas and sequence them to reflect the central conflict, order of events, climax, and so forth. If they write a cause-and-effect essay, they can create a graphic organizer that reflects the connections between ideas. Or they might fashion an outline to show the hierarchical relationship or logical ordering of information.

For arguments or informational essays or reports, allow students time to research and take notes so they can begin to investigate and narrow a topic. Later in the writing process, students will revisit their notes to fashion a thesis and likely determine that more research is required to develop their papers. Organize these notes, and a collection of other prewriting tools, in a physical or electronic writing folder.

Drafting

This stage involves allowing students' ideas to take shape as they consult the materials and resources they created and accumulated during prewriting. The criteria for the writing product introduced earlier via a checklist or rubric (or both) should be visible during this stage so students write with knowledge of expectations, including the task, purpose, and audience. They can compose with pencil and paper or type on an electronic device. Concerns about grammar or conventions—writing mechanics—should not interfere with the fluid thought process that results in a first draft; students can identify and correct any errors later during the editing stage.

In this phase, give students dedicated, uninterrupted time to write. Some will create their first rough draft in a fluid situation, in which they write continuously and then reread their work for clarity while taking notes about what needs improvement. Others might jot down notes that spontaneously surface for areas needing future revision or editing. Still others will draft sections and then stop at points to conduct more research or gather information if prewriting failed to yield enough material. Since the writing process is recursive, it is wholly plausible that writers will return to the prewriting tools when composing first and subsequent drafts. No way is right or wrong; it's purely a stylistic approach to drafting.

Revising

During revision, students correct major errors to improve the development and content of a draft. They shouldn't concentrate on fixing grammatical and spelling errors; that happens later, during editing. The primary goal of the revision stage is to step back and look objectively at the content of the paper as readers to self-assess and evaluate what works and what doesn't. When revising, it is critical to solicit and collect feedback from peers, teachers, and invested individuals outside the classroom. Armed with their self-evaluation and input from others, writers can make conscientious and informed adjustments to their second (and subsequent) drafts for refinement and perhaps further development. Since writing is an iterative process, students may revise more than once during the course of working on a comprehensive paper, and the number of drafts is individualistic.

There are a host of revisionary options, such as adding, rearranging, changing, replacing, or deleting text based on the task. For example, writers can add more evidence to support an argument, rearrange body paragraphs, change the conclusion to leave a stronger impression, replace weak words with stronger ones, or delete erroneous evidence that does not connect to the thesis. Revision can also mean checking the organization and focus of the paper, ensuring that the facts are correct, replacing overdone language, or adding descriptive details. In some cases, revising might reveal that writers need to generate an entirely new draft.

It is sometimes difficult for students to determine what they need to change or augment to improve their papers. They must understand what revision entails and the possibilities for what and how to revise (Witte, 2013). Therefore, you should explicitly teach students ways to detect and make necessary changes and also indicate how revision differs from editing before students can begin to roll up their sleeves and focus on improving their papers. What follow are some suggestions you may like to implement.

Self-Assessment

Students should take an active role in assessing their own work to identify areas needing further attention. There are different ways to self-assess drafts to pinpoint strengths and weaknesses. A simple example is asking students to read their papers aloud. (This is also a useful technique when editing.) Often, the simple act of reading aloud will reveal unclear or awkward sentences or an argument that is not supported with sufficient evidence. Another option is to put the paper aside for a few hours or days and revisit it later. Taking a break from one's writing allows students to look at it with fresh eyes and reconsider the quality of the work.

Students can also use a rubric formatively to self-assess and score a peer's work. Using a rubric during the revision stage is a wise move, as students can zero in on the writing's strengths and weaknesses. One example of a straightforward way students can capitalize on rubrics to improve their writing is described in the four steps that follow. To model this exercise and others mentioned throughout the book, access student writing models through the links listed in appendix B. (Additional information on rubrics and extensive suggestions for using rubrics as an instructional tool appear in chapter 4.)

1. The student reads his or her own paper, highlighting areas of the rubric indicating scores and associated descriptors reflective of his or her writing. The student stores this marked rubric in a manila writing folder or electronic folder temporarily.
2. The student invites a peer to read his or her paper and also assess it by marking a clean copy of the rubric with a different colored highlighter.
3. The student compares his or her self-assessment scores with those of the peer evaluator. He or she might request a meeting if there are confusing discrepancies in scores that need to be clarified.
4. The student revises his or her work based on this data collection. Additionally, he or she can use the information as the basis for a student-teacher conference if the data give rise to confusing points.

Another formal assessment strategy that yields self-reflective data is a genre-specific revision sheet, like the one for an argumentation piece featured in figure 2.1. You should create a revision sheet specific to the writing type or genre and aligned with the writing checklist and rubric. After the first draft, students assess their own work using the revision sheet to determine if they have satisfied the criteria. To use it, they critically examine their own papers by following the prompts to provide evidence (or a lack of evidence) of key criteria. Peers can also use a new copy of the same revision sheet to assess classmates' papers to offer feedback. It is important to model how to complete the revision sheet first, using sample student work.

You'll notice that the top of the revision sheet includes yes or no responses. The focus, though, is on more revisionary prompts included in the rest of the sheet. For each one, reviewers can respond in one of three ways.

1. **Strong:** If the writer or reviewer can state with conviction that an aspect of the paper is present and done well, he or she enters evidence from the paper along with an asterisk denoting it is strong and fine as is.
2. **Average or weak:** The writer or reviewer recognizes that an element is included, but realizes it is average or rather weak. If this is true, he or she enters the evidence and then puts parentheses around it to indicate that it needs to be improved when revising for the next draft.
3. **Nonexistent:** The writer or reviewer realizes that the element is missing; therefore, the line item remains blank to show it is omitted.

Feedback

Although feedback can be given in other stages of the writing process, it is most prevalent during revision. The goal of written and oral feedback is to facilitate learning by providing students with the input they need so each draft is an improvement on the previous one. It's the critical driver to support students in moving from where they currently are in their learning to proficiency. As John Hattie and Gregory Yates (2014) note, "Receiving feedback enables the learner to close a critical gap, specifically the gap between current status and a more desirable level of achievement" (p. 66).

For feedback to be useful, students need to know what they are aiming for and the tools and information they need to meet goals. According to Hattie (2009), feedback asks, "Where to next?" It should specifically point students in the right direction to progress. It needs to be targeted enough so that they can make changes for improvement as if to say, "I understand and can use this feedback. It gives me guidance and direction to move forward."

Providing students with feedback during the revision stage of the writing process differs from evaluative feedback. The latter is given at the end when students submit papers for a summative assessment and receive a grade. Feedback throughout the process, from prewriting until project completion, is formative—assessment *for* learning, rather than *of* learning. Constructive and timely feedback serves to meaningfully impact and improve students' work as they collect input, review it, and make discriminating revisions that incorporate these comments.

<table>
<tr><th colspan="3">Argumentation Revision Sheet</th></tr>
<tr><th>Descriptor</th><th colspan="2">Circle</th></tr>
<tr><td>The writing genre is an argumentation essay (or literary critique or argumentation speech).</td><td>Yes</td><td>No</td></tr>
<tr><td>The paper stays on topic and focuses on one overarching claim.</td><td>Yes</td><td>No</td></tr>
<tr><td>There are no grammatical or convention errors; the paper is properly formatted.</td><td>Yes</td><td>No</td></tr>
<tr><td>Each paragraph is correctly indented.</td><td>Yes</td><td>No</td></tr>
<tr><td>There is an original title that captures the intent of the argument.</td><td>Yes</td><td>No</td></tr>
<tr><td>The paper maintains a consistent and appropriate point of view.</td><td>Yes</td><td>No</td></tr>
<tr><th>Descriptor</th><th colspan="2">Idea Development and Organization</th></tr>
<tr><td>The introduction provides context and engages the reader.</td><td colspan="2">Write a sentence or two from the introduction that shows context and engagement.</td></tr>
<tr><td>There is a clearly stated thesis to stake a claim.</td><td colspan="2">Write the thesis statement.</td></tr>
<tr><td>The writer states logical and specific reasons to support the thesis. The reasons are expressed as topic sentences.</td><td colspan="2">Write the reasons that support the claim.</td></tr>
<tr><td rowspan="2">There is relevant and sufficient evidence throughout the paper to build a logical argument.</td><td colspan="2">Check all that apply:
❒ There is relevant and sufficient evidence in all body paragraphs.
❒ It's hard to see how the evidence in paragraph ____________ relates to the reason or reasons.
❒ More evidence is needed in paragraph ____________.</td></tr>
<tr><td colspan="2">Comments:</td></tr>
</table>

Figure 2.1: Argumentation revision sheet.

continued ➤

<table>
<tr><td rowspan="5">Each reason (topic sentence) is supported by evidence and elaboration.</td><td>Write the three strongest pieces of evidence.</td><td>Enter elaboration for the evidence.</td></tr>
<tr><td>1.</td><td></td></tr>
<tr><td>2.</td><td></td></tr>
<tr><td>3.</td><td></td></tr>
<tr><td colspan="2">Comments:</td></tr>
<tr><td rowspan="2">The paper acknowledges and addresses the opposing viewpoint.</td><td colspan="2">State an acknowledgment of an opposing viewpoint.</td></tr>
<tr><td colspan="2">Write a reason for countering the opposing viewpoint.</td></tr>
<tr><td>A strong conclusion sums up the major points and leaves an impression on readers.</td><td colspan="2">Write a sentence that sums up the overriding argument or leaves a lasting impression.</td></tr>
</table>

Descriptor	Language and Style
The paper includes accurate and strong **words to support the argument**.	Write at least four strong words relevant to the argument. They may be discipline related.
The paper maintains a **formal style and objective tone**.	Write two sentences indicating appropriate style and tone for the audience. 1.
	2.
Descriptor	**Transitions and Sentence Structure**
Transitions connect ideas so the paper flows from sentence to sentence within a paragraph and also from one paragraph to the next.	Write three transitional words or phrases used to connect sentences.
	Write transitional words or phrases that connect paragraphs.
Sentences **begin in different ways**.	Write two sentences that each begin in a different way. 1.
	2.
Sentence structures vary.	Write two sentences that each have a different sentence structure. 1.
	2.

Source: Adapted from Glass, 2013.

Visit ***go.SolutionTree.com/literacy*** *for a free reproducible version of this figure.*

Feedback is criteria based since the revision is guided by standards-based expectations articulated on a checklist or rubric. For example, a comment might indicate that more appropriate transitions are needed to make the writing more fluid, or that topic sentences must be revised to support the thesis statement (or vice versa). Students not only use the feedback to improve their work and capability, but by examining students' work to offer input, it compels you to identify the degree to which students are mastering skills and adjust your teaching as needed. When you provide and orchestrate feedback opportunities all throughout the writing process, the work that students ultimately produce is likely strong.

There are many who can and do provide feedback: teachers, classmates, peers from within the school, fellow writers in a digital community, parents or guardians, family members, and so forth. As well, students can ask for and receive feedback in multiple ways. They can do so verbally through face-to-face communication, or they can capitalize on the rich electronic and digital options available, such as using an audio-capability tool, participating in an online writing community with members of a public or controlled private group, or chatting via Skype or Google Hangouts. The online options—with classmates they know or with other invested writers they have never met in person—can contribute to student engagement and motivation. They also provide a venue for working outside the classroom on a schedule conducive to students' individual lifestyles (such as late at night or on weekends).

Reviewers need to learn constructive ways to give feedback. For example, however well-intentioned they might be, comments can backfire if presented incorrectly. Furthermore, input should be geared toward informational feedback that students can use to push learning forward, rather than toward praise. Hattie and Yates (2014) find that "praise is not a strong source of reinforcement" and does not "serve as a viable facilitator in academic classroom learning" (p. 68). When teaching and providing feedback, abide by the following key elements from Grant Wiggins (2012) to help students improve. Feedback must be:

- **Goal referenced**—What is the goal of the feedback? How will it help accomplish a task? Additionally, what are the criteria against which students can self-assess and critique peers' work? For example, "Transitions between sentences are one of the goals of this assignment and is listed on the rubric. These particular words and phrases make writing flow and help eliminate choppiness. Reread your paper, and determine where you need to add transitions to accomplish this goal."
- **Tangible and transparent**—The feedback must be clear and obvious so students can understand what it means and can actually use it as a learning tool. Writing comments such as "awkward" or "wrong word" can confuse students, who may skip over the input because they do not know what it means.
- **Actionable**—Rather than commenting in nebulous ways like "Nice job!" or "You missed the mark," augment those phrases with specific and useful feedback. That can mean reinforcing what works so students can continue to implement a skill and pointing out what didn't so they can revise. For example, explain the impression the writing has on the reader: "The dialect you wrote in your story's dialogue helped me to identify the region the character's from and understand his bias." Or, "Your paper includes many similes. In the middle of the story, they were distracting to me as a reader and felt overdone."
- **User-friendly**—Consider your students and use language that they can understand when providing feedback. Furthermore, do not overwhelm them by offering too much at once, which might derail students.
- **Timely**—Throughout the writing process, provide feedback in a timely manner so students can apply the input as soon as possible to their drafts. If feedback is given after they've turned in a published piece, they cannot learn from salient comments that may contribute to improvement. Timely feedback can come from myriad individuals—peers, those outside the classroom, and you.
- **Ongoing**—Integrate continuous opportunities for feedback orally, in writing, and through electronic means from self-assessments, peer critiques, an online community, parents or guardians, and you as the teacher. In this regard, the ongoing

nature of feedback is built into the writing process not just during revision—where it is most typical—but also in other stages, as appropriate.

- **Consistent**—Use rubrics and collect anchor papers that show different performance levels of criteria items so there is consistency about what constitutes quality. Train students in how to deliver consistent feedback. As well, teachers across a school and district should work together to score student work to avoid differing impressions of quality and to operate from a shared understanding of what meeting standards looks like. (See also the sections on Identifying Anchor Papers and Calibration in chapter 4, page 70.)

Feedback can come from a number of valuable sources. Peer, parent or guardian, and teacher feedback are all beneficial to students.

Peer Feedback

It is incumbent on you to teach students how to give and receive feedback so they use it as intended: to propel learning. Share Wiggins's (2012) aspects of feedback along with the following suggestions to guide students in offering productive input. During participation in critical peer assessment, a natural byproduct is that students can learn how to improve their own writing by critiquing and providing suggestions to others about their work.

- **Be respectful:** Explain to students that their goal is to provide constructive feedback in a courteous way that supports the writer's work. Explain how to tactfully and respectfully give comments and, if needed, how to show interest by maintaining eye contact and positioning their bodies toward one another to invite discussion.
- **Use the checklist or rubric criteria to focus feedback:** Conduct a whole-class lesson on a particular skill featured on the checklist or rubric using anonymous student writing samples. Find samples that illustrate strong and weak examples of the skill, and model how reviewers can make associated comments. (See chapter 4 for resources on locating sample student work and more instructional suggestions.) As practice, ask students to give and receive feedback on each other's papers based on this key skill. Remind them that the basis for their feedback emanates from criteria pieces and that each feedback session should begin by stating the purpose for the feedback.
- **State strengths first:** Have students read the whole paper or section. Although constructive feedback is critical, it is also important to identify the writing's merits first before jumping into what needs improvement. Students can comment using any of these sentence starters to prompt them.
    - "My overall impression of this paper (or section) is ____________________."
    - "The part I find most interesting is ____________________."
    - "From this paper (or section), I learned ____________________."
- **Offer constructive feedback:** Here are additional examples from those presented previously that reflect tangible and actionable comments.
    - "The beginning engaged me as a reader. When I got to a sentence that I thought was the thesis, it was weak and could've been stated more clearly."
    - "I am confused about the audience you are addressing because the paper changes points of view throughout the piece."
    - "The story is in sequential order, and I can follow each event well. It's not as suspenseful as it could be since I don't feel much tension as I read events climbing to the story's climax."
    - "The counterargument you provide sways me to the other side without bringing me back to yours."

    Also, consider providing students with these feedback sentence starters. Tie the comments to the criteria on the checklist or rubric.

    - "This part is most confusing because ____________________."
    - "I think the paper is missing ____________________."

- "My most important suggestion for revision is ____________________."
- "I'm still wondering about ____________________."

- **Suggest resources:** Encourage students to reference a lesson you have conducted and any resources provided during teaching as they relate to revisionary suggestions. For example, a peer reviewer can provide feedback about the types of evidence (such as statistics, testimony, and examples) his or her partner uses to make an argument and may also suggest a handout, textbook page, or Internet link as a resource for revision.
- **Remember whose paper it is:** Mention that the writer has the ultimate authority on whether to accept any feedback. Just because peers (and other reviewers) provide input does not mean the writer has to incorporate each comment into the paper.

Before teaching what it means to engage in feedback sessions, build a sense of community to invite sharing in a nonthreatening and supportive way. Be prepared for students who are reluctant to share. Talk with them to determine what is preventing them from showing their work to others. It could be their papers aren't developed enough, they might be second language learners and insecure about certain skills, or maybe the content of the paper is sensitive or personal. Assist these students to shape their drafts to the point that they are more receptive to sharing, and help them select peers who might be better suited to provide the input they need.

As receivers of feedback, students have a specific role, as well. Consider sharing these pointers with your student writers as they collect input. Students should:

- **Confirm that the feedback addresses the criteria**—Explain that students should identify how the feedback relates to the expectations from the checklist or rubric or perhaps goes beyond them.
- **Determine if the feedback is sufficient and clear**—Make sure students know how to use the feedback to improve their writing. If not, they should ask for additional information or clarification.
- **Listen to the feedback and take notes**—During oral sessions, taking notes ensures students interpret the feedback others offer as it was intended. Even orally summarizing or repeating what students hear from a reviewer can help them collect the necessary feedback. Students can use a sentence frame, such as "I heard you say . . ." to confirm their understanding.

Logistically, devise a system in the classroom in which students sign up for support when they are at the point in their writing where they need feedback from peers. Include an option for students to indicate how many peers they want involved in listening and giving feedback, such as one on one or in a trio. You may consider using a sign-up sheet to match writers to reviewers. The sign-up sheet can allow students to specify the kind of information they are requesting peers to target when they review, such as word usage, evidence, organization, and so forth. (Again, these emanate from the genre-specific rubric or checklist.)

If a writer meets with a small peer-review group, he or she can assume the role of facilitator. As writers listen to others, they can take notes by hand or on the computer, or even audio record the session to review later, so remind students to come to the meeting prepared. Students can also exchange their writing pieces and make comments on sticky notes to affix to specific places in the text where input is warranted. Additionally, if the goal is digital feedback, like through Google Docs, students can determine if they want voice responses or typewritten ones.

Designate a part of the room where conferences can take place. If students work with one or two others and hold a discussion or if they record their comments orally on a device, advise them to lower their voices to be mindful of those around them who are writing. Consider having noise-canceling earphones or earplugs available to students who are bothered by ambient noise. In the classroom, there's bound to be chatter if students are conferencing together or recording comments into a device. Of course, if students are providing input by handwriting or on their electronic devices, the noise factor is diminished accordingly.

Parent or Guardian Feedback

Sometimes well-intentioned parents or guardians like to give feedback, but their interference can have a detrimental effect. When they make corrections or rewrite parts of students' papers instead of allowing students to detect and correct their own errors, it doesn't serve anyone well. In this kind of situation, you don't have the advantage of learning where students' deficits and strengths lie so you can address them. Parents who assume an imposing stance hinder students from learning how to write, and this can become an exercise in frustration for you and students. Consider providing guidance to your students' parents or guardians to supply constructive feedback so they can productively partner with you in their child's learning. To do so, send home figure 2.2 (page 26), "Suggestions for Parents or Guardians in Assisting Student Writers."

Teacher Feedback

You play an active role in helping students progress through the writing process and improve their work. Contribute to this process by giving sound feedback that provides a sense of clarity and spurs further refinement and development of students' papers. Refer to the characteristics of feedback in the earlier section to ensure that your comments have a high likelihood of efficacy. Match your input to students' skill levels. Hattie and Yates advise (2014), "Different types of feedback work best depending on the individual's phase of learning—corrective feedback is suited for novices, process feedback is needed as the learner becomes proficient, and elaborated conceptual feedback becomes effective with highly competent students" (p. 66).

Conduct short conferences and circulate around the room to briefly connect with each student. Begin by asking them to identify where they might need help, or merely pose a general question, such as, "How is your paper going?" "Is there a challenging or confusing part that you want me to read?" "Are you stuck somewhere?" or merely, "How can I help you strengthen this paper?" On a recordkeeping sheet, keep track of students you didn't visit during the class period, and be sure to touch base with them the next day or time the class meets. Record reminders to circle back with all students after providing comments to check on their progress.

Lead with something positive before sharing weaknesses. Be as detailed as possible so students leave with tangible information they can use for revision. For example, you might say, "The quote you include in this paragraph is particularly compelling. When you revisit your paper, focus on elaboration to explain this evidence more clearly." Or say, "You constructed your thesis statement in an impressive way and take a solid stand. To support it, direct your attention to crafting stronger reasons to be more convincing." The first comment stresses a writing strength followed by a suggestion for improvement. Avoid the word *but*, such as in the sentence, "Your dialogue shows the interaction between characters well, *but* you haven't included strong speaker tags." Uttering this tiny word can result in the student negating the positive comment stated before the conjunction.

However, beginning with the positive doesn't always have to be the case, especially when you establish a strong rapport with your students, they are familiar with conferencing, and something clearly needs revision. Nancie Atwell (2015) asserts that it is permissible to be forthright about what doesn't work well:

> Don't hesitate to be direct, as long as your response is specific. It's okay to say to a student, "I'm lost," "I'm confused," or even "I'm having a hard time caring about this." But you need to follow up with *why* and *what the writer can do* to address the problem. (p. 213)

Also pose questions to target students' needs and activate new thoughts and directions. By doing so, you can help empower them to arrive at their own solutions to obstacles they face in their writing. You are aiming for the *aha* moment when students indicate they know where to take it from here. Consider asking these kinds of questions; then follow up with concrete suggestions if students are floundering for support.

- "Have you considered rearranging any (or this) part of your paper? How might that change your work?"
- "What impression do you want to leave on readers? Do you feel your conclusion does this?"
- "Can you provide elaboration on what you've written here? What do you mean to say that maybe isn't worded in the way you'd like or that got you stuck?"
- "Which reason is the most convincing in your argument? Do you have enough evidence to support it properly?"
- "Is all this dialogue meaningful to the story, and does it move the plot forward? Where do you feel you might delete some of it?"

Dear Parent or Guardian,

I am invested in helping students become better writers. In order to do this, I need to gauge each student's writing ability so I can build on his or her strengths and address weaknesses. Many parents choose to partner with teachers to help students in this endeavor. Following are suggestions for you to support and help improve your child's writing skills. Please refrain from writing on your child's paper; instead, offer feedback using these pointers as a guide. In doing so, you empower your student writer to arrive at his or her own ideas for revision, which will contribute to his or her achievement and ability to self-assess. Feel free to attach a note with any specific comments or questions you have about the writing that your child can address in class during peer or teacher conferences.

1. **Focus on the assignment task and expectations:** Ask to see the assignment sheet, checklist, or rubric. Review the task and criteria with your child to clarify a particular assignment's expectations. Encourage him or her to ensure the paper addresses all parts of the writing assignment and criteria.

2. **Recognize proper organization:** Ask for evidence of proper organization of the whole paper and within paragraphs based on the genre of the piece. Look at the checklist or rubric to guide this discussion, and ask questions such as the following.
   - "Are you writing a story? If so, is there a logical sequence? Have you included plot elements, such as a central conflict, rising action, a climax, and so forth?"
   - "Is this an argumentation essay? If so, can you show me your thesis statement that stakes a claim? Are your reasons in a logical order? Do your reasons and evidence support your thesis? Are there counterarguments? If so, are they well placed to support your argument?"
   - "Are your paragraphs for expository text structured appropriately? Are there a topic sentence, supporting details or evidence, and an ending?"
   - "Do you include text features—such as charts, graphs, a table of contents, subheadings, a glossary, and so on? Let's reread the paper to be sure that these text features help organize the piece."

3. **Consider the development:** Is the paper complete? If it's a story, are characters, setting, and events fully developed? Are narrative techniques included to enhance it (like dialogue and description)? If it is an argument, are there enough reasons, and are there sufficient evidence and elaboration to support each reason? Are counterarguments acknowledged and addressed? Refer to the checklist and rubric to ensure all items have been thoroughly met.

4. **Look at word choice:** Ask your child to do the following.
   - Review the paper and circle words that he or she feels are strong and reflect the best choice. Reread the paper and assist your child to replace any words that could be more precise or descriptive using a print or digital thesaurus (www.merriam-webster.com, www.vocabulary.com, www.collinsdictionary.com, or www.thesaurus.com), classroom textbook, or other resource, as needed.
   - Ensure that the word choice or language is appropriate for the audience.
   - Make sure words are accurately used, including subject-matter terms related to topics or content areas. If they are not, refer your child to an appropriate resource.

5. **Examine sentence beginnings and structure:** Ask your child to read the first three words of each sentence. Ask these questions: "What do you notice about the beginnings of sentences? Are the words and parts of speech different? Do they sound too repetitive?" Ask him or her to revise sentence beginnings, as appropriate, so there is variety. Additionally, discuss sentence structure, and ask if he or she has varied the types of sentences (for example, simple, compound, and complex sentences) so there is a natural rhythm to the writing.

6. **Conduct oral reading to detect convention errors:** Ask your child to read the paper aloud and self-assess by doing the following.
   - *Listen for clarity*—If a sentence is hard to read, it could reflect a grammatical error. Ask him or her to find and correct any grammatical errors.
   - *Listen for natural stops or pauses*—When there is a natural stop, ask if there is proper end punctuation (a period, exclamation mark, or question mark). This will also help to detect run-on sentences or fragments that need fixing. If there is a pause, inquire whether a comma or end punctuation mark is needed and what rule might apply.

Figure 2.2: Suggestions for parents or guardians in assisting student writers.

To be realistic, there is not time during the class period to read or listen to each student's whole paper, especially lengthy ones. Not only is that improbable, but in a differentiated classroom, students are working at different paces and need feedback at pivotal times in their own writing cycles. Outside of class time, read or skim students' papers and comment on them online (if using a digital community), or share your observations in person the next day in class. If students have a particular area that needs more attention than what you can provide during class, invite them to request more feedback. Specifically, ask them to prepare questions or indicate confusing or fuzzy parts of their papers that beg input. When you read the student's paper, direct your attention there.

Aside from keeping track of conferences on the record-keeping sheet, also record and review individual and collective observations and comments about student writing. This data can help you determine next steps to differentiate instruction. You might learn that several students need support in a particular area, so you can pull a small group to reteach or emphasize certain skills. As well, you might discover that some students need enrichment.

Editing

This is the proofreading stage in which writers focus on improving their piece's readability and accuracy. Once the paper includes the desired content and development, writers edit by attending to proper grammar and usage as well as the mechanics of writing, also known as *conventions*—capitalization, punctuation, and spelling—and formatting—margin widths, font size, and Works Cited document details. Include the grammar and writing conventions that students need to address in the writing checklist and rubric, which should align to grade-level standards. In the Common Core, standards related to the aforementioned areas are located in the Language strand, which also includes vocabulary acquisition and usage (National Governors Association Center for Best Practices & Council of Chief State School Officers [NGA & CCSSO], 2010).

Make resources available to students so they can make editing corrections. These can include online links to the Modern Language Association (MLA) or American Psychological Association (APA) format styles, dictionaries (www.merriam-webster.com, www.vocabulary.com, or www.collinsdictionary.com), or other reference materials.

Questions related to grammar and usage, conventions, and citation and document format can guide students' editing. This stage focuses more on functional and basic changes like questions related to sentence structure (Are my sentences complete?) and word choice (Do I delete or replace repetitive words?). With regard to sentence syntax involving rearranging parts of sentences for stylistic effect or adding descriptive detail, those decisions are more revisionary. Figure 2.3 (page 28) contains a partial list of questions for editing.

As with revision, an effective way to help students spot grammar or mechanics errors is to recommend that they read their writing aloud. When doing so, they might see that a sentence is awkwardly written or a word is missing and then fix it. The caution, however, is that sometimes it is easy to automatically fill in missing words by accident, so students should not rely solely on this method for proofreading. Another editing technique is to read the paper backward to spot misspelled words.

Students cannot edit each other's papers effectively unless they are taught to do so; therefore, model how to edit for specific grammar and writing conventions properly. After employing direct instruction on a particular skill (such as complex sentence construction or pronoun antecedent agreement), ask students to apply what they learn to a peer's paper and eventually their own. As part of the lesson, introduce the standard proofreading symbols and teach students to use them to mark editing errors on a hard copy. Table 2.1 (page 29) includes a list of these marks and examples for how to use them.

Publishing

When students publish their work, use the genre-based rubric they received at the beginning of the unit to score this culminating assessment. (See chapter 4 for a discussion about grading.) If students have diligently followed the writing process steps, including incorporating constructive feedback from you and others, their grades or comments should not surprise them. In fact, students should fare quite well. Consider inviting them to improve their grades through another revision and to turn in their papers again if they are not satisfied with what they earned. Remember that the ultimate objective is for students to synthesize the skills they've learned all unit long to progress in their writing so they produce a sound, well-developed piece. If they choose to return to their work and revise, applaud them for having the

Conventions

- Do I use proper conventions for titles? Are appropriate words either lowercased or capitalized? Do I use italics, underlining, and quotation marks correctly?
- Are there words that seem to be misspelled that I need to check and correct?
- Do I include appropriate paragraph breaks?
- Do all compound sentences include either a comma before the coordinating conjunction or a semicolon to separate the independent clauses?
- Do I use commas correctly in all instances—for example, in a series, after a dependent clause that begins a sentence, to separate coordinate adjectives, to set off appositives, and so forth?
- Are my end punctuation marks correct? Is there an unnecessary repetitive use of exclamation or question marks?
- Do I use correct conventions when writing dialogue between two or more speakers?
- Do I use quotation marks correctly for excerpted material?
- Do I use single quotation marks when including a quotation within a quote?
- Do I use ellipses correctly when omitting a word, phrase, or paragraph from a quoted passage?
- Do I place apostrophes in the right spot to show possession, or do I need to add them?
- If I include parentheses, brackets, hyphens, dashes, or semicolons, do I use them correctly?

Grammar and Sentence Structure

- Do I use consistent verb tense throughout my paper?
- Do all my subjects agree with the verbs?
- Do I avoid run-on sentences and sentence fragments?
- Do I use consistent point of view, or do I need to replace any pronouns?
- Do I have proper pronoun and antecedent agreement in gender and number?
    - Gender agreement examples: Marshall delivered his speech. Kimmie told her friends she would arrive late.
    - Number agreement examples: If a student [singular] is tardy, he or she [singular] needs a pass. When women [plural] receive equal pay as men for the same work, they [plural] will rejoice.
- Do I use active instead of passive voice, as appropriate? (*Active:* Mike reluctantly completed his household chores. *Passive:* The household chores were reluctantly completed by Mike.)
- Do I use correct parallel sentence structure?
    - *Correct:* Lucy loves <u>playing</u> volleyball, <u>baking</u> cookies, and <u>creating</u> art designs. *Incorrect:* Lucy loves playing volleyball, baking cookies, and when she goes swimming.
    - *Correct:* Daren said her daughter's shorts are too <u>tight</u>, <u>skimpy</u>, and <u>inappropriate</u>. *Incorrect:* Daren said her daughter's shorts are too tight, skimpy, and didn't want her wearing them.

Format

- Do I correctly use in-text citations to give proper attribution to sources I use?
- Have I formatted my Works Cited document appropriately?
- Does my paper reflect the correct format with regard to margins, word count, headings, and so forth?
- If my paper is handwritten, is my writing legible?
- If my paper is typewritten, do I use an appropriate font, type size, and ink?

Figure 2.3: Questions to ask when editing.

Table 2.1: Proofreading Marks

Mark	What It Means	How to Use It
	Delete a letter, word, or phrase.	Harryy Potter was was sorted into Gryffindor.
∧	Insert a letter, word, or phrase.	Ron Wesley was also in Gryffindor.
⊙	Insert a period.	Professor Snape didn't like Harry He gave him lots of homework.
	Insert a comma.	King's Cross Station is in London England.
|#	Insert a space.	Hermionehad very bushy hair.
	Insert a quotation mark or an apostrophe.	“Happy Christmas, Harry, said Ron.
	Delete space; close up the gap.	Harry a nd Ron were mad about Quidditch.
	Delete and close the gap.	Ron had a pet rat named Scdabbers.
¶	Begin a new paragraph.	“He's not Fred. I am,” said George. “Just kidding,” said Fred.
	Run up; keep sentences in the same paragraph.	Ron couldn't wait to get to dinner. He was positively starving.
	Transpose; switch words or phrases around.	Ron and Harry both were thrilled to be back at Hogwarts.
≡	Capitalize a letter, word, or phrase.	Hermione granger was the smartest girl in the class.
/	Make this lowercase.	Harry's Uncle despised magic.
○	Spell this out.	His 2 favorite teachers were Professor Dumbledore and Professor McGonagall.
stet	Let it stand; do not change.	Use when a proofreading mark is incorrect.

desire, perseverance, and diligence to make additional adjustments and resubmit their work.

Publishing can also involve sharing the final product with a wide variety of individuals and groups and in several different forms, depending on the task, purpose, and audience. The possibilities are endless; you may like to ask students for their ideas in addition to considering these.

- Members of the school community, such as peers or younger students outside the classroom, classmates within the classroom, teachers, the principal, or school board members
- School publications, such as an article in the school newspaper, literary magazine, yearbook, or classroom anthology
- Readers of a print or online newspaper or magazine in the local or city area
- Community members—for example, public officials or businesses
- Those who participate in online writing environments; see the Digital Environments section for a partial list of options
- Publications that sponsor poetry or prose contests or accept submissions, like Teen Ink (www.teenink.com); the Learning Network, a blog based on content from the *New York Times*; and others. See Essay Contests and Submissions in the appendix for a more comprehensive listing of ways to publish publicly.

For sharing in a public forum, inquire about obtaining any necessary permissions. Within the classroom, create opportunities for students to view each other's work to extend their learning on a particular topic. For example, set up small groups, instruct students to swap papers and read them silently, and then discuss their impressions or ask questions. In this regard, they can share finished products with students who were not their peer reviewers. For those who were peer reviewers, this gives them an opportunity to read the final paper with classmates' suggestions included. Another option is to instruct students to summarize their papers and present a speech to the class. They might even create a video or condense their papers to create a PowerPoint, Prezi, or Keynote that highlights the major points of an informational or argumentation essay. After students share their work, assign a debriefing exercise in which everyone writes about what he or she learned from each classmate.

Reflecting

This last stage of the writing process is sometimes overlooked; however, it is worthwhile for students to reflect on what they learned about themselves as writers, collaborators, and even researchers. Pausing after a writing unit, semester, or trimester, or even at the end of the year to debrief, reflect, and record can help students cement insights that inform future writing projects, take stock of their growth, and validate themselves as writers. If you haven't included this step before, review the options in this section. Do not overwhelm yourself or students by asking for too much at first. Perhaps begin by asking a few questions they can reflect on based on one unit. Later you can add a portfolio option as students become more familiar with reflection.

At the end of a particular writing project, consider these and other questions students can answer about their performance and mindset.

- How did I use the strategies of the writing process? Did I miss any steps, or do I wish I had spent more or less time on any? How did the process help me?
- What knowledge did I glean from the topic that I investigated or argued? How can I use this knowledge in my life and in the future? How did it add to or confirm what I already know or change my understanding or beliefs?
- What insights did I gain about myself as a writer during this writing unit?
- Where did I get stuck, and what did I do to overcome this obstacle? Or what helped me to persist?
- During peer or teacher review, what feedback was most helpful to me and why?
- When I reviewed classmates' papers to give feedback, what did I learn that I could apply to my own writing? How can I do a better job of helping classmates improve in their writing next time I participate in peer review?

- If I chose to invest more time in this writing product, what would I want to revise or add? Would I want to write a follow-up piece?
- What would I want to tell next year's teacher about my writing abilities?

If students have stored their work electronically or in hard copies in a writing folder, consider instituting portfolios to help students reflect on their work. There are many advantages to this kind of project, such as tracking and noticing growth, comparing burgeoning expertise in particular genres, and creating goals as writers. To undertake this venture, students judiciously select a collection of choice pieces at the end of a semester, trimester, or year based on criteria you can provide. For example, they can include not only polished, finished writing pieces but perhaps a graphic organizer they feel is particularly detailed, a rough draft that showcases substantial progress in the development of a paper, or an interview they conducted to provide evidence. Arrange dedicated time for students not only to gather these items but also to write, type, or orally record reflections about them. Provide guidelines for evaluating or annotating selected pieces—for example, an explanation for why each item or a compilation of similar items is noteworthy or meaningful. Or students can respond to selected queries like the ones that follow, those presented earlier for unit reflection, ones you devise, or others that they create.

- Why specifically did I choose this piece?
- What is the strongest aspect of this piece?
- What part of this piece do I wished I spent more time on?
- How does this piece show my improvement? In other words, how does this piece reflect my beginning knowledge as a writer that has now grown?
- How does all or part of this piece reflect a risk that I took?
- Where is a place that shows I incorporated feedback from someone?
- How does this piece show an example of how I've emulated a writer's style?

Consider posing questions that are not necessarily tied to a particular piece students insert in their portfolio but that provide a reflection in general. For example, you might ask them to respond to these kinds of questions.

- When I look back on my experience as a writer, what genre had the most influence on my writing and why?
- What genre or element of a genre do I need to further experiment with to become more proficient at it?
- Which authors most influenced me as a writer?
- Which topics most intrigued me or made me think more deeply?
- What are my future goals as a writer?

Additionally, give direction on organizing and assembling (such as, "Should there be a cover letter and table of contents?"); plus, feature examples of portfolios, and offer ways that students can share theirs. For instance, they can lead a parent-teacher conference in which they use their portfolios as the focal point for discussion about their improvements and what they plan to focus on in future writing projects. Or invite parents or others close to the student into class and host a sharing party. Students can also submit a portfolio for high school or college purposes, or share them with classmates. Students can take advantage of various technological options for reflections and portfolio projects. They can save, compile, share, and record digitally on electronic devices, which is the subject of the next section. If you do decide to use portfolios (electronic or not), communicate to students the purpose the portfolio will serve so they can plan accordingly which pieces to include. The portfolio's purpose might be to showcase students' best work in a unit, reflect growth over time, identify strengths and weaknesses, demonstrate mastery of certain skills, show evidence of the writing process, serve as an assessment tool for a course or semester, or a combination of the aforementioned.

Using Digital Environments During the Writing Process

Aside from using pencil and paper, various types of technology, including typing on an electronic device or using video or webpages, pervade writing at different stages of the process. To support composing in multiple environments pertaining to electronic technologies, allow students to access and utilize apps and online tools. For example, students might draw, type, or speak using a web-based app or program that enables them to brainstorm in all sorts of ways during prewriting. A class might participate in an online community to make writing and collecting input authentic and engaging. Perhaps students could take advantage of a learning management system (LMS) where courses are housed. Within such a system, discussion boards can be created and serve as a means for students to give and receive feedback.

This section contains a list of resources you may find useful at various points in the writing process. As you read about the resources, determine how best to use the online tools and apps. For example, Notability is a note-taking app that students can use as they research and collect information individually during prewriting, but they can also access it again during drafting when they need to conduct further research. Additionally, combining apps and web tools can prove beneficial. For instance, you can provide options for note taking and then extend the possibilities by sharing tools for giving audio feedback to the notes students take.

Many tools have capabilities beyond those described in the list. There are several variables to consider, so conduct your own research to vet and select appropriate tools. For example, determine if any options look viable for classroom use based on the devices and technology available, as some tools are cloud based, some are only for iOS, and others are only for Android. Also, consider the content-area standards you are accountable to meeting, your students' characteristics and needs, and your budget. Certainly consider the Children's Online Privacy Protection Act (COPPA, 1998), which states among other legalities, "While children under 13 can legally give out personal information with their parents' permission, many websites disallow underage children from using their services altogether due to the cost and work involved in the law compliance." Therefore, some websites are not suitable for students under the age of thirteen.

Take some time with any apps before using them in a classroom. When presenting them to students, provide an introduction or a review about how to access and use them to their advantage. Consider asking students who are familiar with a particular digital tool to teach their peers how to use a certain app, since many are extremely tech savvy. Of course, solicit technology personnel at your school or district to assist you. In fact, ask colleagues and even students who are familiar with the latest technology to recommend other tools. Additionally, conduct your own online search to learn about other options, read reviews, collect information, and stay abreast of technology standards. Google Drive and Google+, for example, have a vast array of tools at teachers' disposal—Google Docs, Google Hangouts, Google Sheets, and so on. Here are some of the undoubtedly many available links to assist that search and keep you up-to-date on what is new.

- Alice Keeler (http://alicekeeler.com)
- EdTechTeacher (http://edtechteacher.org)
- Educational Technology and Mobile Learning (www.educatorstechnology.com/p/teacher-tools.html)
- Edutopia (www.edutopia.org)
- Free Technology for Teachers (www.freetech4teachers.com)
- Graphite (www.graphite.org)
- International Society for Technology in Education (ISTE; www.iste.org/resources)

Online tools and apps are ever changing. New tools come on the market, and some are no longer available by the time people read about them. Therefore, what I present here is a partial collection—feel free to add to it. The tools in the sections that follow are organized into categories. Many have widespread usages; the category corresponds with the most prominent feature of each tool or app. If one piques your interest, I encourage you to investigate it by going to the applicable website and learning about all the capabilities in addition to the ones I mention here.

- Individual writing tools and apps
- Collaborative writing tools and apps
- Conceptualizing tools and apps
- Tools for organizing, collecting, and archiving work
- Tools for engaging others
- Tools for presenting information
- Tools for managing learning

Visit **go.SolutionTree.com/literacy** for a list of all the following tools, including their categories.

Individual Writing Tools and Apps

Although these tools have collaborative capabilities, first consider ways to use them during the writing process where students generate work independently. Then introduce collaboration at a suitable time during the process.

- **Blogs:** Students can create personal, classroom, or school blogs to share their writing. For example, they can post drafts and invite others to comment or engage in discussion around the written piece and also publish their finished work. Teachers can create a blog and share it; students can also have their own blogs and use them only in the classroom. As always, be mindful of COPPA restrictions. A blog can only be used by the person who is assigned to it. Some sites, like Populr.com, allow collaboration on an interactive blog. Consider the following blogging platforms: Blogger (www.blogger.com), WordPress (www.wordpress.com), Edublogs (www.edublogs.org), Kidblog (www.kidblog.org), Glogster (www.glogster.com), or Google Sites.
- **Infographics:** Infographics are visual images that represent information or data graphically so that what is displayed is quickly understandable even at a glance. They allow students to share a message, simplify a presentation that includes large amounts of data, convey statistical information, navigate from one place to another (think subway map), or ascertain data patterns and relationships. Students already use many kinds of infographics—for example, bar graphs, pie charts, histograms, tree diagrams, and so forth. With this technology tool, students can, for example, research and synthesize information and then create and present an infographic to demonstrate what they have gleaned. Try Piktochart (https://piktochart.com), Infogr.am (www.infogr.am), Easel.ly (www.easel.ly), or Venngage (www.venngage.com).
- **Note-taking tools:** There are several digital tools available to use for note taking. They can serve as organizational tools to use when researching. Students can create a research notebook and share it with teachers. While researching, they can create a new note for each source and include appropriate citations, pictures of excerpts from paper resources, screenshots, and even a summary to explain how they'll use the content. Students can also tag notes with subheadings, such as *Introduction, Thesis, Evidence, Reason One, Reason Two,* and so forth. Try the following.
    - *Evernote (www.evernote.com)*—Evernote allows students to upload notes as well as photos, documents, audio files, or presentations that can be accessed or shared on any device. Users can efficiently view, replay, share, or search notes.
    - *Microsoft OneNote (www.onenote.com)*—Microsoft OneNote looks like a traditional notebook for students to write notes or ideas, grab screenshots, or make lists. Any notes users write on an interactive whiteboard can be inputted directly into a shared student notebook, and teachers or students can edit the text concurrently.
    - *NoodleTools (www.noodletools.com)*—This is a research management tool with integrated capabilities for note taking, outlining, citation, document archiving and annotation, and collaborative research and writing. The note-taking system supports paraphrasing, summarizing, direct quoting, and analyzing what students read. Teachers have access to what students produce and can interact at any time along the way.
    - *Notability (www.gingerlabs.com)*—Notability is a note-taking app that allows teachers and students to share and organize notes and even annotate PDFs in writing or audio recordings. Users can add images and other media, plus draw diagrams, make charts, and crop images to fit a particular project. Notes can be exported to various online sources.
- **Note-taking feedback tools:** Teachers or students can comment on students' work simultaneously in real time. For example, teachers can encourage students to recategorize their notes, add more detail, or double-check their facts. Try the apps AudioNote and SoundNote for this opportunity to extend the note-taking process. Each app syncs audio recording with what the user types or draws on screen.

- **Publishing tools:** Using the educators' version of Weebly (www.weebly.com) allows teachers to create an account and provide free web space for students to create and publish various products, such as interactive websites for their local and global peers and electronic portfolios.

Collaborative Writing Tools and Apps

In a writing unit, students will ultimately produce their own finished products. (In other units, they might generate a culminating project in a pair or with a small group.) However, there is a definite collaborative element all throughout the writing process on their way toward publishing the final piece. For example, during prewriting, students can bounce ideas off each other, or they might share resources and discuss options for devising search queries. While sharing and revising, students provide and solicit feedback from teachers, classmates, and others who respond in writing or through voiceovers in digital communities. Consider using the following tools and apps for collaboration.

- **Google Docs:** Students can compose a piece of writing on a Google Doc for a variety of purposes. During brainstorming, students can generate a document and invite others to add ideas. During the revising or editing stage, peers and teachers can have immediate access to the writer's document to make comments by writing in a text box or highlighting text. With Google Docs, during or after students write, others can make comments in real time. Google Docs automatically saves changes, and only users granted permission can do so. Aside from written comments, teachers and peers can also leave verbal comments (like a voiceover) that writers can play back; search for *Kaizena* under the Add-ons in the toolbar to access this option. Google for Education even offers a version where students (particularly younger ones) don't need an email address. If you go this route, students have an account, but the email functionality is turned off. You or a technology supervisor can regulate the accounts.
- **Amazon WorkSpaces (https://aws.amazon.com/workspaces):** Amazon has a similar service to Google Docs allowing usability among people. It provides users access to each other's documents, applications, and resources.
- **Explain Everything (www.explaineverything.com):** This interactive screencasting whiteboard has many capabilities. Any file can be uploaded and accessed, and then teachers or students can use their own voice to record feedback or annotate on the selected file and share it with selected peers. Or students can share their screen with a classroom projector so many can view it simultaneously as the basis for discussion.
- **Kami (formerly Notable PDF; www.kamihq.com):** Kami is a cloud-based all-in-one office productivity tool. Students and teachers can view, annotate, and share files online.
- **MindMeister (www.mindmeister.com):** This tool is a collaborative online mind-mapping software that offers real-time brainstorming sessions among an unlimited number of users. The maps can be shared and published to the web or embedded on blogs and websites. Students can also use this software to take notes, manage information, and study content.
- **Scrible (www.scrible.com):** This tool lets users highlight and annotate webpages and easily save, share, and collaborate on web research with others.
- **Wikispaces Classroom (www.wikispaces.com/content/classroom):** Wikispaces Classroom is a social writing platform where teachers and students can communicate and work on writing projects alone or in teams. Teachers have access to assessment tools to measure students' contributions in real time. Teachers and students can give feedback and assistance.

Conceptualizing Tools and Apps

When students first begin their work, they need to envision what they are going to create based on the prompt. They conduct research, think and mull over ideas, and ultimately prewrite so they can plan. Here are some digital tools to help them with idea generation in the prewriting stage and throughout the process as necessary.

- **Ideament (formerly Idea Sketch; www.nosleep.net):** During prewriting, students can use this app to create diagrams on their iPads, such as mind maps, concept maps, or flowcharts. There's a feature that allows users to convert their diagrams to a text outline, and vice versa. They can save and share their diagrams and outlines, plus copy text from an email, document, or webpage and import it.
- **Inspiration (www.inspiration.com):** This is a software program that enables users to create visual maps to brainstorm ideas, take notes, structure and organize information and writing, and create presentations. There are more than one hundred graphic organizer templates available across content areas.
- **Popplet (www.popplet.com):** Students can use Popplet to generate and manage ideas by creating a platform for brainstorming, recording notes, and organizing the information in a usable way.

Tools for Organizing, Collecting, and Archiving Work

Throughout the writing process, students gather information and generate work that together contribute to the finished writing product. Consider these tools to support students with organizing what they accumulate—research notes, website links, graphic organizers, drafts, and so forth—and to store these items by electronically filing them. They can also use these applications to share work for a variety of purposes.

- **Google Sheets:** Google Sheets is an online spreadsheet app for creating and formatting spreadsheets. It allows users to simultaneously work with others to update and edit information. For a writing project, students can enter and organize sources or data they have researched or vocabulary words they want to incorporate into their work. Importing, converting, and exporting to and from formatted data are possible.
- **Google Forms:** With this app, teachers can plan, poll, survey, quiz, or merely collect information. They can create a Google Form from scratch or from an existing spreadsheet in Google Sheets and manage the responses. To view the responses, users can elect to see them as a summary, individually, in spreadsheet form, or downloaded as a file.
- **LiveBinders (www.livebinders.com):** This is a site that has tools for curating—pulling together, sifting through, and selecting—digital content and sharing it with others. It features a digital three-ring binder that can house a wide range of content, such as webpages, PDFs, documents, images, or videos. Students can share their binders via Twitter, Facebook, or Google+ or embed them into a website or blog.
- **Electronic portfolios:** Electronic portfolios make it possible for students to capture, share, and reflect on evidence of their learning and growth over time. In their customized portfolios, they can share images, videos, documents, presentations, or any representation of their progress and pride. Teachers can comment on their work as well. Try Pathbrite (https://pathbrite.com), Taskstream (www1.taskstream.com/solutions/eportfolios), and Educlipper (https://educlipper.net). Additionally, teachers may also consider asking students to create a portfolio to display their work by generating a website through Google Sites. They can then share their portfolios with classmates, school groups, audiences in other states or countries, and other readers. The University of Wisconsin–Stout (www2.uwstout.edu/content/profdev/rubrics/eportfoliorubric.html) offers a rubric to assess digital or e-portfolios or adapt for portfolios generated with hard copies.

Tools for Engaging Others

Teachers can use social media and online groups collaboratively or as learning tools. Note that many social media sites will not allow students under age thirteen to have a user account. Consider privacy issues, and teach students how to sensibly use the sites you recommend and the purpose for engaging in these digital venues.

- **Google Communities:** Google Communities is an online platform for people who have common interests, like food, music, or sports. Students can join a community based on their writing topic to learn information, get inspiration, share ideas, or collect feedback on drafts.

- **Figment (www.figment.com):** This site is a free online community designed for young adults and teens to create and share their writing and discuss their favorite works. Students can compose, comment, and collaborate in a private group composed of their peers and teachers at different stages in the writing process. Teachers can post and update assignments, share links for resources, show writing samples, and monitor and comment on student work. Teachers can also model a writing skill through discussion, ask students to practice it, and provide feedback. A group discussion tool allows for online participation in a class discussion where students can ask questions and share resources.
- **Social media platforms:** Twitter (https://twitter.com), Facebook (www.facebook.com), Snapchat (www.snapchat.com), and Tumblr (www.tumblr.com) allow users to post text, photos, quotes, links, music, and videos from their browsers, phones, desktops, or emails. For example, students can share ideas they are considering developing and post links of their work to ask for feedback from an audience that is wider than their classroom and teacher.

Tools for Presenting Information

Consider using apps and electronic tools to capitalize on the Speaking and Listening standards from the Common Core English language arts (ELA) standards and expectations that are similar in other state or province documents. In doing so, you give students the opportunity to share their work with various authentic audiences who can learn from their material. In addition, you can use these apps as vehicles to create and present lessons and content to your students.

- **Adobe Spark (https://spark.adobe.com):** This app allows users to devise animated narrated videos using an inventory of available images, icons, themes, and music or to use words and images to create magazine-style web stories. Once students finish their writing product, they can use this app to formally present the most important points of their work. They can then share their presentations live in front of the class, through social media, or via a link to parents and other audiences. As with any of the apps in this category, you can use this as a teaching tool to share content and teach skills.
- **Google Slides:** An online presentation app through Google Drive, Google Slides allows users to create, edit, and display their work visually and insert images and videos. Users can import existing files and convert them to Google Slides.
- **Haiku Deck (www.haikudeck.com):** Users can access innumerable decks (a set of slides like in a PowerPoint), templates, and images to create presentations on the web, an iPad, or an iPhone.
- **ShowMe (www.showme.com):** ShowMe enables iPads to be converted into personal interactive whiteboards. You can record voice-over lessons and share them with your class or a global community of fellow educators and students. Examples of what other teachers have created are housed on the website for anyone to access. (Choose wisely, as they are not vetted for quality.) Additionally, students can create their own presentations to share with the class based on their writing products.

Tools for Managing Learning

Teachers, administrators, parents, and students can connect via an educational platform that connects everyone with each other or selected groups within a network. Many possibilities are available with these learning management systems depending on the organization you choose to tap. You can customize the capabilities of the system to involve students and parents, as appropriate, for these types of functionalities.

- Assign tasks and provide links to differentiate learning for individuals or groups of students.
- Assign homework.
- Issue quizzes.
- Post lectures or videos.

- Manage and share students' progress.
- Insert links of pertinent documents and resources.
- Facilitate blended or distance learning.
- Make collaborative learning synchronous.
- Annotate student work.
- Create online classes with discussion boards for peer and teacher review.
- Orchestrate collaboration.
- Post classroom or school notices.

Here are some of the many systems you can investigate for more details on their offerings: Blackboard (www.blackboard.com), Canvas (www.canvaslms.com/k-12), Edmodo (www.edmodo.com), and Moodle (https://moodle.org).

Summary

To support students in acquiring writing skills, explicitly teach the strategies associated with the stages of the writing process—prewriting, drafting, revising, editing, publishing, and reflecting. Early in the process, clearly identify and communicate the assignment's task and criteria students are expected to master for a particular writing assignment via a checklist or rubric.

Within your lessons, incorporate published work and student samples so students have an opportunity to examine and identify strengths and weaknesses of various aspects of a paper. By detecting and articulating what works and what doesn't in others' writing, they can improve their own writing skills.

Formative feedback aims to help students reduce or eliminate the void between where their writing currently is and where they need to be based on criteria expectations. Engineer situations for students to receive feedback from a variety of individuals—themselves, peers, you, and others—in person and perhaps through digital venues. Teach students how to give and receive constructive, effective feedback. Target your comments and probing questions according to the scoring criteria, and avoid praise, as it can dilute the positive effects of learning and lead to lower engagement and effort (Hattie, 2012). Share feedback while students are writing instead of saving comments until the end when their papers are ready to be published.

As students move through the stages of the writing process, capitalize on myriad apps and tools available that are compatible with the devices they are using. This can support and enhance their writing and also contribute to more authentic audiences and tools that are emblematic of the digital environment inside and outside the classroom.

The next two chapters are dedicated to an explanation of a backward design approach to use when devising writing units. I present each component of the approach along with some examples.

CHAPTER

3

The Backward Planning Approach to Unit Design: KUDs and Guiding Questions

When planning any unit of instruction, there is an orchestrated method to help ensure that optimal learning takes root. This chapter introduces the components of backward planning in general and focuses on the first stage of this research-based design process.

Essentially, *backward planning* is the practice of designing units by beginning with the learning outcomes and what constitutes success in a final product before creating specific lessons. When starting with a clear focus on goals and evidence of learning, you can be more intentional in lesson planning so each lesson has an express purpose to support overarching unit goals. Teaching in this manner has proven to optimize the likelihood for success. For example, John Hattie (2009, 2012), renowned synthesizer of more than eight hundred meta-analyses, cites in his seminal work *Visible Learning* that backward planning is a sound pedagogy that correlates and contributes to an increase in student achievement. As Grant Wiggins and Jay McTighe (1998) state:

> Why do we describe the most effective curricular designs as "backward"? We do so because many teachers *begin* with textbooks, favored lessons, and time-honored activities rather than deriving those tools from targeted goals or standards. We are advocating the reverse: One starts with the end—the desired results (goals or standards)—and then derives the curriculum from the evidence of learning (performances) called for by the standard and the teaching needed to equip students to perform. (p. 8)

In backward design, the initial step, which is the focus for this chapter, is to identify the results expected of students. To formulate these learning outcomes, begin by grouping all the content-area standards together for a particular unit. Then, identify what you want students to *know* (knowledge items), *understand* (essential or enduring understandings), and be able to *do* (skills). These components are commonly referred to as *KUD*s (know, understand, and do). Succinctly stated, knowledge indicates the rudimentary, surface items that students should know as a foundation. Essential understandings are conceptual statements that emanate from these factual pieces of information. Skills signify what a learner is expected to actually do and acquire; they represent complex processes that are taught and measured. Using KUDs, you can devise unit-level guiding questions to frame instruction on a conceptual level, which can then be further broken out into discrete lesson-guiding questions.

Using the desired goals as a guide, the second phase involves designing a culminating assessment task with accompanying criteria to enable students to show evidence of meeting the targeted results. The last stage—planning differentiated learning experiences that include additional assessments—is designed by focusing squarely on the KUDs and guiding questions, which will prepare students for completing the culminating assessment. The specifics about teaching methods, the order of presenting each lesson, ways to differentiate, resources, assessments, and other decisions are more effective and targeted once a clear vision of goals and successful evidence of meeting them are in place. Figure 3.1 illustrates all the components of backward design in unit planning.

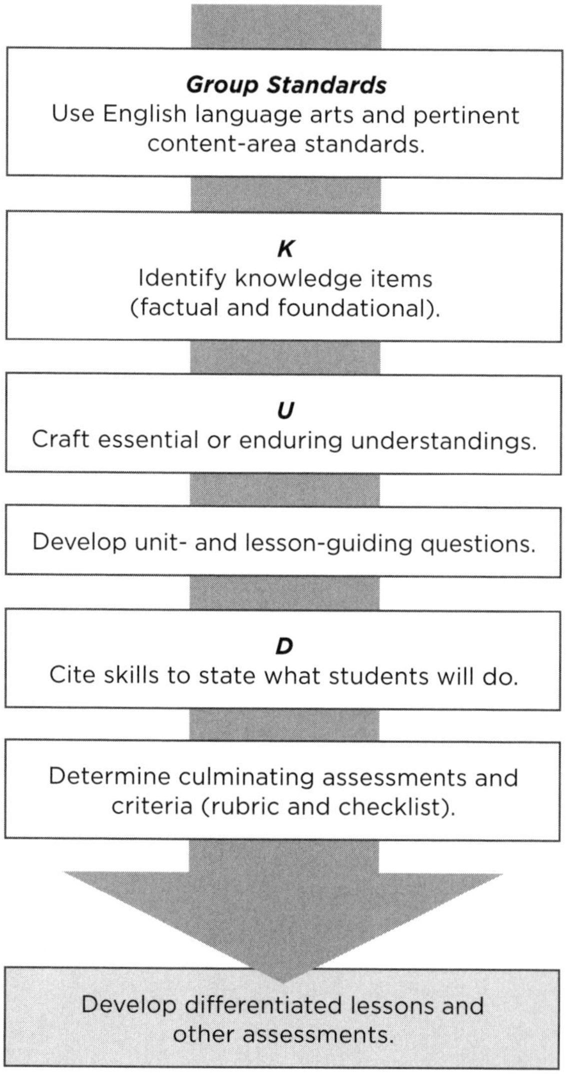

Figure 3.1: Unit-planning components of backward design.

Each component of backward planning works smoothly with the others to fashion a fully developed and intentionally rigorous unit of instruction. Although featured in a linear sequence in figure 3.1, you can rearrange and address KUDs and guiding questions in a different fashion as you toggle back and forth between them working to design learning outcomes in preparation for lesson design. For example, you might move between them as thoughts emerge to record in the moment, if you're stuck and need to generate new ideas, or if you want to brainstorm in many areas and then revisit each component carefully. No matter the order in which you devise the KUD components and guiding questions, ensure that content-area standards guide the unit.

Creating a Unit Template

When developing your unit, you can create a unit map using a unit map template, like in figure 3.2, that includes all the facets of backward planning. The map, which focuses directly on standards-based learning goals, will be your guide for devising differentiated lessons. As you read this text and access pertinent figures and tables available at **go.SolutionTree.com/literacy**, you'll be well positioned for (re)designing your own writing units.

Identifying Group Standards

When designing or redesigning a writing unit, first group together targeted standards per your district, state, or province. The standards specify a writing type to be the center of instruction, such as these for argumentation and persuasion. The following are examples of ELA standards you might encounter when developing your unit.

- Common Core English language arts standard, grade 6 (W.6.1; NGA & CCSSO, 2010): Write arguments to support claims with clear reasons and relevant evidence.
    a. Introduce claim(s) and organize the reasons and evidence clearly.
    b. Support claim(s) with clear reasons and relevant evidence, using credible sources and demonstrating an understanding of the topic or text.

Unit: ______________________________

Subject: ____________________ Grade: ____________

Time Frame for Teaching Unit: ____________

Standards	Knowledge Items	Essential Understandings	Unit-Guiding Questions	Lesson-Guiding Questions	Skills
Culminating Assessment (Writing Task):					

Figure 3.2: Unit map template.

Visit ***go.SolutionTree.com/literacy*** *for a free reproducible version of this figure.*

c. Use words, phrases, and clauses to clarify the relationships among claim(s) and reasons.

d. Establish and maintain a formal style.

e. Provide a concluding statement or section that follows from the argument presented.

- Virginia's English Standards of Learning (SOL), grade 11 (Virginia Department of Education, 2010):

a. Generate, gather, plan, and organize ideas for writing to address a specific audience and purpose.

b. Produce arguments in writing that develop a thesis that demonstrates knowledgeable judgments, addresses counterclaims, and provides effective conclusions.

c. Organize ideas in a sustained and logical manner.

d. Clarify and defend position with precise and relevant evidence elaborating ideas clearly and accurately.

e. Adapt content, vocabulary, voice, and tone to audience, purpose, and situation.

- Texas Essential Knowledge and Skills (TEKS), grade 6 (Section 110.18; Texas Education Agency, 2015):

(18) Writing/Persuasive Texts. Students write persuasive texts to influence the attitudes or actions of a specific audience on specific issues. Students are expected to write persuasive essays for appropriate audiences that establish a position and include sound

reasoning, detailed and relevant evidence, and consideration of alternatives.

Some standards documents, such as those mentioned previously, include a fair amount of specificity regarding the type of writing to be taught. Others—for instance, those from Ontario—offer suggestions but not mandates of writing formats, as shown in this grade 8 example:

> Write complex texts of a variety of lengths using a wide range of forms (e.g., a memoir of a significant Canadian; a report comparing the economies of two nations and explaining how a new industry might affect each nation's economy; briefing notes for an oral debate outlining both sides of an argument, including appeals to both logic and emotion; etc.) (Ontario Ministry of Education, 2006, p. 145)

When locating standards on which to base a writing unit, do not stop at just the standard that mentions the actual genre or writing type (for example, argument, narrative, informational). There are others related to processes and strategies to supplement the writing piece, so make sure to locate and group those together; for example, employ the writing process, establish a central idea, organize and develop ideas and information, identify purpose and audience, collect information from multiple researched sources, use clauses and phrases for sentence variety, and so forth.

Other language arts standards that support writing are also important to flag. Therefore, consider pertinent reading as well as speaking and listening standards that you should target collectively for a particular genre. For example, Common Core anchor standard eight for reading is altogether aligned with argumentation writing: "Delineate and evaluate the argument and specific claims in a text, including the validity of the reasoning as well as the relevance and sufficiency of the evidence" (CCRA.8; NGA & CCSSO, 2010). This grade-level reading standard would support a unit on narrative: "Analyze how complex characters (e.g., those with multiple or conflicting motivations) develop over the course of the text, interact with other characters, and advance the plot or develop the theme" (RL.9–10.3; NGA & CCSSO, 2010). Sometimes standards for research and technology are embedded within a Writing strand; however, some documents feature them in their own section, so be sure to augment your unit map with these pertinent standards. As well, do not overlook any standards associated with grammar and conventions. In the Common Core, they are located in the Language strand.

Also include content-area standards for content areas other than language arts, as they apply. If students write an argument based on subject-matter content (like global warming or Supreme Court appointments), include content standards (from areas like science or social studies) to account for discipline-related material. Similarly, if students are writing an informational report or historical fiction piece on a period in history, such as the American Revolution or medieval Europe, include associated standards in your unit map.

Establishing Knowledge Items

The next step in the backward design approach is to identify knowledge items. Knowledge items are the factual and foundational things we want students to know. Specifically, these are the facts, terms, people, places, examples, or dates associated with a unit; however, not all units include each of these items. Knowledge items do not begin with verbs because this would reflect what we want students to *do* (which is discussed in the section on skills). Rather, knowledge is what we want students to *know* and can be represented in list form, on a graphic organizer (such as steps in the writing process or causes and effects of the Civil War), or by a diagram (such as the digestive system or car engine parts). You can generate these lists, organizers, or diagrams yourself, or you might pull an existing resource previously created or use one that is available online or in a textbook.

Sometimes creating a list of desired knowledge items takes a long time. This can happen when you are not familiar with the content you need to teach, perhaps because you are new to the profession or have switched to a different grade. In this situation, research information, peruse available materials, or even take a class to become proficient in the content. Another scenario that requires time for compiling a knowledge list is when you want to incorporate a new resource into the curriculum or your district adopts a new textbook, in which case you'll need to first review the unfamiliar resource or text carefully before identifying knowledge items. See figure 3.3 for examples of knowledge items for three sample writing units.

Writing Focus	Knowledge (Students will know . . .)
Transitions	• Purpose of transitions • Categories (*time, place, comparison, clarification*) and specific transitional words and phrases (*subsequently, whenever, in similar fashion, to clarify*) • Appropriate transitions to use to connect sentences within a paragraph for fluid thought and reading • Appropriate transitions to use to logically and cohesively connect ideas and sections within a paper
Figurative Language	• Types of figurative language: simile, metaphor, imagery, personification, and hyperbole • Definitions and examples of figurative language • Reasons authors use figurative language and its intended effect • Inferences and multiple meanings
Argumentation Introduction	• Introductory parts: hook, context, and thesis • Hook options • Context for argument • Thesis statements: purpose, structure, and placement in introduction • Thesis statement: the author's overarching claim that states a position; must be based on a debatable issue rather than something accepted as a fact (such as, *Air pollution is bad for the environment*) • Writers may revisit and revise their introductions throughout the writing process.

Figure 3.3: Excerpts of knowledge items from sample unit maps.

Crafting Essential Understandings

As mentioned earlier, knowledge items include facts that reflect surface and foundational learning; these facts are often tethered to a particular unit in a specific grade. Essential (or enduring) understandings, however, are broader and deeper generalizations. They represent what we want students to understand in the long term, encapsulate the essence of a unit, and emanate from the standards and the knowledge list. These lofty statements rely on *concepts*, which are defined as a "one- or two-word mental construct that is broad and abstract, timeless, universal, and represents a variety of examples that all share the attributes of the concept" (Erickson, 2002, pp. 69, 74). Concepts, which are expressed as nouns, can be linked to a subject area, such as *diversity* or *cultural diffusion* for social studies, *energy* or *organism* for science, or *exposition* or *literary devices* for language arts. *Macroconcepts* are those terms that reach across several disciplines, such as *change*, *system*, *structure*, and *perspective*.

Essential understandings should be transferable across time and cultures and predicated on introspective concepts (like *global economy*, *perspective*, *patterns*, and *intolerance*) that convey significant ideas. Therefore, more than one grade level can conceivably share the same essential understandings since they are expressly designed for idea transference and connections. To enable this flexibility, avoid the use of proper nouns or past-tense verbs that would anchor the essential understandings to a particular time frame, situation, or individual.

To connect the concepts in an essential understanding, use strong verbs other than forms of *to be* (*is*, *are*, *was*, *were*). This way, the depth increases, as verbs can carry profound meaning (such as *change*, *form*, *invent*, *establish*, *create*, and so forth) along with the concepts. Many sentences sound like statements of fact when using forms of *to be*, which would place them in the knowledge category instead of the category of essential understandings. For example, *Biographies are nonfiction pieces a biographer writes about someone else's life* is a fine sentence, but not strong enough for an essential understanding and instead reflects a fact you want students to know. This, however, is an essential understanding: *Biographers can uncover obstacles people face, reveal their strengths, and inspire readers.* Both knowledge and essential understandings are needed in a unit map; they each serve a different and important purpose in unit design.

Figure 3.4 continues the sample excerpts of unit maps from figure 3.3, this time illustrating how essential understandings correspond to them. As you peruse it, focus on the connection between the knowledge items and essential understandings.

The rationale for developing and using essential understandings to plan units of study is well founded (Erickson, 2007). These understandings represent the conceptual insights and essence surrounding a unit that students should come to realize and retain years later, even after specific facts might be lost. However, students will likely remember seemingly disparate and isolated facts more if they connect them to concepts and essential understandings. In fact, Lynn Erickson (2007) states that the "synergistic interplay between the factual and conceptual levels of thinking" is critical to intellectual development (p. 2). Further, she writes, "When curriculum and instruction require students to process factual information through the conceptual level of thinking, the students demonstrate greater retention of factual information, deeper levels of understanding, and increased motivation for learning" (p. 2).

If your unit is interdisciplinary (for example, requiring students to write about a science or history topic), develop some essential understandings pertaining to the content area and others pertaining to the English

Writing Focus	Knowledge (Students will know . . .)	Essential Understanding (Students will understand that . . .)
Transitions	• Purpose of transitions • Categories (*time, place, comparison, clarification*) and specific transitional words and phrases (*subsequently, whenever, in similar fashion, to clarify*) • Appropriate transitions to use to connect sentences within a paragraph for fluid thought and reading • Appropriate transitions to use to logically and cohesively connect ideas and sections within a paper	Proficient writers use appropriate and varied transitional words and phrases to form logical connections among ideas, create cohesion, and contribute to fluid reading.
Figurative Language	• Types of figurative language: simile, metaphor, imagery, personification, and hyperbole • Definitions and examples of figurative language • Reasons authors use figurative language and its intended effect • Inferences and multiple meanings	Writers invent (*create, compose*) figurative language to convey fresh insights that readers interpret to deepen and extend meaning.
Argumentation Introduction	• Introductory parts: hook, context, and thesis • Hook options • Context for argument • Thesis statements: purpose, structure, and placement in introduction • Thesis statement: the author's overarching claim that states a position; must be based on a debatable issue rather than something accepted as a fact (such as, *Air pollution is bad for the environment*) • Writers may revisit and revise their introductions throughout the writing process.	Compelling introductions provide a foundation for an argument and offer context that establishes the importance of the issue, makes a favorable impression, and clearly articulates a position.

Figure 3.4: Excerpts of essential understandings from sample unit maps.

language arts standards. As mentioned, deep understandings transfer, so consider using them across grade levels, units, and subjects, if they apply. For example, this essential understanding for ancient China can be used for other civilizations: *As civilizations evolve and become more complex, they develop different structures and systems to meet their ever-changing needs, which impact society then and now.*

Developing Guiding Questions

Unit- and lesson-guiding questions set the purpose for learning and connect to the essential understandings and knowledge items. Whereas the essential understandings are written by and for teachers, the guiding questions are in student-friendly language. Although all questions direct learning, unit- and lesson-guiding questions each have their own characteristics. Unit-guiding questions are broad and provide an overarching focus that promotes higher-level thinking (for example, *How does figurative language enhance writing?*). The lesson-guiding questions detail a series of graduated steps that are necessary to master the unit question and encompass skills. By the time you have taught all lessons associated with each lesson-guiding question, students should be able to answer the overarching unit-guiding question. The following figures (figures 3.5, 3.6, and 3.7) present the unit-guiding questions, lesson-guiding questions, and skills (discussed later) for the knowledge and essential understandings introduced in figures 3.3 and 3.4.

Notice that the unit-guiding questions are overarching and provoke critical thinking for the unit's major concepts, so they begin with open-ended words such as *how* or *why*. In addition, they are global and transferable and—similar to essential understandings—can apply to different units of study. Some examples across content areas may include these: *How can human interaction affect the environment? Is conflict avoidable? How can economic reasoning be used to make decisions about scarce resources? Is obesity a government issue? How does the writing process contribute to optimal products? Should teachers require students to read the classics?*

An additional characteristic of unit-guiding questions is that each essential understanding holds the answer to a corresponding question. For example, the unit-guiding question *How does elaboration facilitate understanding?* can have this accompanying essential understanding: *Through elaboration, writers provide commentary, interpretation, or discussion about their selected evidence so readers can follow their thought process in support of a position.*

Knowledge (Students will know . . .)	Essential Understanding (Students will understand that . . .)	Unit-Guiding Question	Lesson-Guiding Questions	Skills (What students will do)
• Purpose of transitions • Categories (*time, place, comparison, clarification*) and specific transitional words and phrases (*subsequently, whenever, in similar fashion, to clarify*) • Appropriate transitions to use to connect sentences within a paragraph for fluid thought and reading • Appropriate transitions to use to logically and cohesively connect ideas and sections within a paper	Proficient writers use appropriate and varied transitional words and phrases to form logical connections among ideas, create cohesion, and contribute to fluid reading.	Why and how do writers use transitions effectively?	• Why do writers use transitions? What are some examples of transitions in (name the text)? • How can I use transitions within paragraphs to make my (argument, short story, other text) flow? • How can I use transitions to form logical connections among ideas in my (argument, short story, other text)?	• List and categorize transitions. • Use transitions in writing to reflect text structure.

Figure 3.5: Sample KUDs and guiding questions for a unit map excerpt (transitions).

Knowledge (Students will know . . .)	Essential Understanding (Students will understand that . . .)	Unit-Guiding Question	Lesson-Guiding Questions	Skills (What students will do)
• Types of figurative language: simile, metaphor, imagery, personification, and hyperbole • Definitions and examples of figurative language • Reasons authors use figurative language and its intended effect • Inferences and multiple meanings	Writers invent (*create, compose*) figurative language to convey fresh insights that readers interpret to deepen and extend meaning.	Why and how do writers use figurative language?	• What are types of figurative language? What are examples of metaphor (simile, imagery, and so forth) in (name the text)? • Where does (name the author) use metaphor? What is being compared? What can we infer from this comparison? • Where is an appropriate place in my (mystery, memoir, other text) to use figurative language? Which type should I use? How can I construct a thoughtful metaphor (or other form of figurative language)?	• Define terms. • Locate and give examples and nonexamples. • Analyze author's craft. • Make inferences and interpret text.

Figure 3.6: Sample KUDs and guiding questions for a unit map excerpt (figurative language).

Thus, while the guiding questions should be visible to students to ground their learning, refrain from sharing the essential understandings in advance of the lessons because students then have the answers. Essential understandings crystallize your thinking and help you focus on the learning outcome. You can then develop learning experiences around these questions to support students in discovering the answers for themselves. If you merely state the essential understandings, students will not have the opportunity to learn for themselves, which they'll gain through the activities and assessments throughout the unit.

You can conduct activities at the end of the unit in which students ascertain the essential understandings based on the learning they acquired. For example, you may ask small groups to brainstorm and record on separate sticky notes different facts and ideas based on the unit. Instruct the groups to cluster notes that share commonalities and create generalizations that meet the requirements of an essential understanding: determine concepts, enable transference across time and cultures (no past-tense verbs or proper nouns), and include strong verbs, rather than forms of the verb *to be*.

The lesson-guiding questions, on the other hand, are tethered to the unit. Therefore, they can contain proper nouns, past-tense verbs, or specific words that anchor and customize them to the content and task students are engaged in. You can scaffold these more specific questions and list them in order for teaching, as shown in figures 3.5, 3.6, and 3.7.

Although lesson-guiding questions set the purpose for learning, it's unnecessary to always present the questions in advance of a lesson. Rather, you might engage students in a simulation, conduct a lab demonstration, show a video clip, or present two examples of student work to compare. With this setup, students participate in an activity or answer a prompt before being presented with the guiding question. For example, you can show two student work examples—one with weak use of figurative language and the other with a strong representation of it. Then ask students, "What do you notice about the differences between these two paragraphs (or papers)?" Elicit responses and then pose the lesson-guiding question: "How can writers use figurative language to develop a vivid setting?" See a synopsis of the major features of both types of questions in table 3.1 (page 48) to guide you in planning your unit.

Knowledge (Students will know . . .)	Essential Understanding (Students will understand that . . .)	Unit-Guiding Question	Lesson-Guiding Questions	Skills (What students will do)
• Introductory parts: hook, context, and thesis • Hook options • Context for argument • Thesis statements: purpose, structure, and placement in introduction • Thesis statement: the author's overarching claim that states a position; must be based on debatable issue rather than something accepted as a fact (such as, *Air pollution is bad for the environment*) • Writers may revisit and revise their introductions throughout the writing process.	Compelling introductions provide a foundation for an argument and offer context that establishes the importance of the issue, makes a favorable impression, and clearly articulates a position.	How can I write an effective introduction for my argument?	• What does an introduction for an argument include? • What is a debatable topic or issue I can use for my argument? What claim can I make? • How do I write a thesis statement to stake a claim? Where should I include it in my introduction? • What engaging strategies can I use to begin my argument? How do I provide a context for reading?	• Identify genre structure. • Choose a debatable or defensible topic. • Discern examples from nonexamples. • Draft an argumentation introduction.

Figure 3.7: Sample KUDs and guiding questions for a unit map excerpt (argumentation introduction).

Citing Skills

What you want students to actually *do* comprises a series of skills that all begin with active, measurable, cognitive verbs (like *define*, *critique*, and *distinguish*), rather than mental verbs (like *understand* and *know*), which are vague and not clearly measurable. You will teach and assess skills directly to be sure students have mastered them with proficiency. Lesson-guiding questions expressly target and address skills. For example, consider these argumentation lesson-guiding questions.

- Why do arguments include opposing viewpoints? How do they impact an argument?
- How do counterclaims, along with reasons and evidence, strengthen a whole argument?
- What are the opposing viewpoints to my claim? How do I acknowledge and address them? Where do I insert counterarguments in my paper?

From these questions, you may target the two desired skills: (1) acknowledge and distinguish the claim from opposing claims and (2) critique and address counterarguments.

Standards are typically expressed as skills, so refer to these documents when creating your desired list of skills. However, there are additional ones you might need to identify to fully cover the unit goals. Consider either the levels of Webb's Depth of Knowledge model (recall and reproduction, skills and concepts, strategic thinking, and extended thinking) or Bloom's revised taxonomy (remember, understand, apply, analyze, evaluate, and create) to pinpoint any extra skills to assess. (See Hess, Jones, Carlock, & Walkup, 2009, for an explanation of both models.) Students need to master certain skills before they learn others, so be mindful to develop all skills in a particular order that reflects a learning progression.

For easy reference, table 3.2 contains a summary of how the standards, KUDs, and unit- and lesson-guiding questions should work together as you design your unit.

Table 3.1: Characteristics of Unit- and Lesson-Guiding Questions

Unit-Guiding Questions	Lesson-Guiding Questions
• Represent an overarching focus, are broad, and foster transference • Begin with *why*, *how*, or *is* to facilitate more open-ended responses, as opposed to a list or yes or no answers • Encompass a series of lesson-guiding questions • Are stated briefly and emanate from a corresponding essential understanding, which provides the answer • Can be used across units of study and grades • Are featured in the classroom throughout the unit on a bulletin board or chart paper to stay grounded in the unit's focus • Form the basis for a culminating assessment	• Are more content-specific and discrete • Address skills • Represent the purpose and focus for a particular lesson • Progress in a particular scaffolded order from basic to more complex • Collectively serve to support students in answering the unit-guiding question, so several lesson-guiding questions are grouped under one unit-guiding question • Are displayed on a whiteboard or interactive board to set the purpose for each lesson during a class period or multiple class periods • Form the basis for formative assessments

Visit ***go.SolutionTree.com/literacy*** *for a free reproducible version of this table.*

Collating Curriculum Maps

Yearlong curriculum maps catalog all units of study across grades and subject areas. Articulating KUDs and expectations across a school or district helps you and your colleagues avoid unnecessary overlap or redundancies and detect absences in content so students' learning experiences are progressive, rigorous, and continuous. There are different formats and templates districts can use to develop a curriculum map. These templates include key curricular components that you incorporate in your unit map—standards, essential understandings, knowledge items, skills, and assessments. Eventually, a more mature map can provide guiding questions, differentiated lessons and activities, and resources. Also recall the discussion in chapter 1 about developing a writing continuum to map genres across grades and subjects. Writing continuums can be nested in a greater yearlong curriculum map.

Collaboration is integral to the creation of a curriculum map document so there is consistency across grades for horizontal alignment and also continuity vertically from grade to grade. A natural outgrowth of such a project is for educators to create unit maps, as featured in this book (see figure 3.2, page 41), and with time eventually (re)design an inventory of comprehensive units of study across content areas to realize the map's intent.

Summary

For any unit of instruction, it is effective to use backward design. Clearly delineate learning outcomes by identifying what students should know, understand, and be able to do related to the content-area standards. Create a unit map using the template featured earlier in the chapter in figure 3.2. Begin by inputting these initial components—recapped in table 3.2—for your targeted writing unit to set the groundwork for deliberate and rigorous curriculum and instruction.

- Grouped content-area standards
- Knowledge that represents the factual and foundational items related to content
- Essential (or enduring) understandings that foster transference and represent the significant principles of a unit
- Guiding questions that set the purpose for learning and are in student-friendly language
- Skills that signify cognitive processes and are directly taught and assessed

Chapter 4 will go into more detail regarding the second stage of the backward planning approach, which involves determining a culminating assessment that displays evidence of understanding along with criteria to assess the product.

Table 3.2: Recap of KUDs and Guiding Questions

Standards	Knowledge Items	Essential Understandings	Unit-Guiding Questions	Lesson-Guiding Questions	Skills
Enter your CCSS or other content standards from your district, state, or province.	List or create a graphic organizer or diagram of what you want students to know that includes any or all of these: facts, terms, people, places, examples, and dates.	Use the standards and knowledge items to create conceptually based statements that get at the essence of what you want students to understand on a deeper level. These are general statements that include concepts, transfer across time and cultures (so they can be used across units and grades), and utilize strong verbs.	Create unit-level guiding questions that are overarching and conceptual. They are briefly stated, are open-ended, and pique interest. The answer to each is an associated essential understanding. All guiding questions are written in language accessible to students.	Create a scaffolded series of lesson-level questions that enable students to answer a unit-guiding question. Each question targets a skill.	List the skills students will learn to do. These are cognitive processes and taught explicitly and assessed. Each skill begins with an actionable verb (such as *list*, *define*, *critique*, *cite*, *distinguish*, and *write*).

CHAPTER

4

The Backward Planning Approach to Unit Design: Pre- and Culminating Assessments and Criteria for Success

Once you articulate a unit's learning outcomes by identifying what students should know, understand, and do (KUDs), it is time to determine how students will show evidence of learning—the second part of backward planning. The focus of this chapter is on the culminating assessment and the criteria against which it will be assessed. Additionally, I suggest ways you can preassess to gather useful information about students' writing capabilities and genre knowledge. I feature tools and strategies for you to create or redesign writing prompts, checklists, and rubrics and discuss writing models, anchor papers, and grading. This culminating assessment and the accompanying criteria, together with the KUDs, will guide you in orchestrating learning experiences to teach key skills. During lesson planning—the last stage of backward planning—you'll have the opportunity to incorporate appropriate resources, instructional strategies and methods, differentiation, and various assessments, implementing all of these with a clear focus on helping students achieve well on the culminating assessment. If needed, review figure 3.1 on page 40 for a visual representation of backward planning to guide your reading of this chapter.

Defining Culminating Assessments

Throughout a unit of study, students should build expertise and capacity until they eventually produce a *culminating assessment*—a type of performance assessment that provides evidence of student learning throughout the unit. According to the Stanford Center for Assessment, Learning, and Equity (SCALE, 2015), performance assessments ask students "to think and produce and demonstrate learning through work authentic to the discipline or real world." Performance assessments have the following four key principles (SCALE, 2015). They:

1. Target skills and knowledge that matter
2. Are assessments *for* and *of* learning
3. Link curriculum, instruction, and assessment
4. Are learning by doing

There are four different types of performance assessments that vary in range according to the complexity of the text and the depth of learning. Specifically, they differ in the number of skills they target, the amount of teaching support required to complete the performance, their opportunities for students to make choices, the fixed or open quality of their finished product, and how long students have to produce the assessment. You select and issue different performance assessments, which can be formative or summative, for various purposes throughout the year. The distinctive quality and effectiveness of performance assessments is that:

> [They] can have the potential to spur learning and not just measure it. Some assessments are just *of* learning. Their sole purpose is to measure whether a student knows or understands something specific. And while performance assessments do need to yield reliable, actionable data about student performance, we purposely talk of performance assessments as assessments *for* and *as* learning. (Dr. Chung Wei in SCALE, 2015)

The first type, the brief *constructed-response assessment*, allows you to glean information fairly quickly about students' abilities or knowledge and is usually administered in less time than a typical class period. This assessment, which is the least complex among the four, can be conducted during or at the end of a unit to gauge what students have learned. For example, provide a prompt along with a reading excerpt or graphic, and ask students to use it as the basis for a response, allowing you to assess students' understanding of one or two targeted skills or concepts.

The *stand-alone performance assessment*, the second kind, occurs as a national or state- or district-mandated assessment to evaluate students for placement or accountability. Examples of this assessment include an advanced placement (AP) test and an on-demand writing prompt that students complete in a finite period of time under a regulated situation, which is characteristic of standardized testing. You could issue a writing prompt in your classroom as a preassessment to determine what students know about a particular writing genre prior to launching into the unit of instruction. As well, you could provide a stand-alone writing prompt at a strategic point during the unit to determine students' understanding of genre elements or structure to gauge your teaching.

Aligned to a particular unit of study that can span several weeks, *curriculum-embedded performance assessments*, the third kind, involve developing and conducting differentiated lessons focused on key skills and measuring multiple outcomes. For example, skills geared for argumentation writing include identifying a defensible topic, researching and synthesizing information, culling evidence, articulating a position, critiquing the credibility of sources, addressing counterarguments, and so forth. Students are granted varying degrees of instructional support to acquire new learning around literacy and subject-matter content. Throughout the unit, they work in different grouping configurations to have opportunities to collaborate with others, but ultimately, each produces his or her own final piece.

A variety of other assessments, specifically preassessments, formative assessments, and self-assessments, yield extensive evidence to plot and monitor growth and ascertain students' ability to apply knowledge and demonstrate understanding specific to the subject matter, topic, and complex text. Therefore, these assessments rely on both *process*—as students are involved in various tasks related to a cross section of reading and writing competencies and those related to subject matter—and *product*—as students work toward a culminating piece. To differentiate, embed ample opportunities for student choice throughout the unit and even in the final task. For example, students might select a topic as the basis for an informational report or choose complex text, pertinent resources, note-taking devices, or grouping situations that meet their needs and learning characteristics. Curriculum, instruction, and assessment are extensively intertwined in curriculum-embedded performance assessments. For our purposes, we will focus on developing a comprehensive unit that could occupy roughly three to six weeks of instruction around this type of performance assessment for writing.

Last, the fourth performance assessment is a *complex project*, which closely aligns to curriculum-embedded assessment. However, it might span a quarter or semester, or account for the coursework in a subject for the entire school year. In short, the four key principles of performance assessments (see page 51) need to be at the forefront of your mind when planning any unit of instruction. Although this book focuses on a written culminating product, other performance assessments can be issued across content areas and are not limited to writing solely. For example, students could write a script and perform a play, choreograph a dance routine, compose a piece of music, or conduct a lab.

Designing Writing Prompts or Tasks

A student's written product provides evidence of learning throughout a unit, as it reflects what he or she has come to know and understand about the reading material and content. When devising a curriculum-embedded performance assessment, fashion a prompt that provides clear and focused direction so students can demonstrate learning based on the standards and learning outcomes. The prompt needs to foster critical thinking and complexity and allow students to apply various reading and writing skills. If the goal is for students to write an argument or informational piece, write the prompt in a way that compels students to showcase their research, analysis, and synthesis from the content related to their writing topic. When designing the task, think of engagement and ways to help students feel invested in their writing. To accomplish this, consider authentic audiences (where students write to a targeted group they can realistically envision). Also provide choice—for example, let students choose an issue, select one prompt from among two or more choices, or focus the writing on self-selected complex texts.

Designing a well-written curriculum-aligned task or prompt can prove challenging. No doubt you, like countless other colleagues, have had the experience of rewriting a prompt over and over to make it just so. You know what you want students to produce, but sometimes crafting a prompt to elicit their best work falls short and appears ambiguous. To frame a prompt well, consider using templates from Literacy Design Collaborative (https://ldc.org/resources#LDC-Task-Template-Collection-3.0). This nonprofit organization offers a collection of K–12 writing frameworks aligned to the argumentation and informational or explanatory Common Core text types that enable educators to issue assignments with clear expectations for and connections between reading and writing standards across grades and content areas. Even if you are in a state or province that does not subscribe to the Common Core, these task templates are worthy of your attention. Literacy Design Collaborative's goal is to provide educators with tools for literacy instruction across core subject areas by integrating reading and writing skill development; their task templates are one resource among many offerings in this area. Figure 4.1 features sample templates and examples of writing prompts using them as a guide.

Writing Templates	Sample Writing Prompts
Task: [Insert optional question] After (reading/researching) _________ (literary texts and/or informational texts on _________ content), write _________ (product) in which you examine causes of _________ (content) and explain the effects of _________ (content). Support your discussion with evidence from the texts.	**What are the effects of hydraulic fracking?** After reading informational texts about fracking, write an informational report in which you examine causes of alternative energy sources, specifically hydraulic fracking, and explain the effects of fracking. Support your discussion with evidence from the texts.
Task: [Insert optional question] After (reading/researching) _________ (literary texts and/or informational texts on _________ content), write _________ (product) in which you argue _________ (content). Support your position with evidence from the texts.	**Should animals be used for scientific or commercial testing?** After researching informational texts on animal testing, write a letter to the editor of the local newspaper in which you argue your viewpoint in response to the question. Support your position with evidence from the texts.
Task: [Insert optional question] After (reading/researching) _________ (literary texts and/or informational texts on _________ content), write _________ (product) in which you explain _________ (content). Support your discussion with evidence from the texts.	**How can writers use authentic cultural characters and conflicts they encounter to foster empathy and realism?** After reading two culturally centered short stories or autobiographies, write an essay in which you explain the experience of the protagonists and address the guiding question. Support your discussion with evidence from the texts.

Source: Adapted from Literacy Design Collaborative, 2014.

Figure 4.1: Sample task templates and prompts.

*Visit **go.SolutionTree.com/literacy** for a free reproducible version of this figure.*

A student checklist and scoring rubric will accompany your prompt. These tools should detail the particular skills students need to demonstrate and reflect clear expectations for the comprehensive writing piece so students are positioned for success. They also serve to keep you grounded in what you're teaching so you are always focused on outcomes. Use KUDs to help develop these items. You might prefer to generate the checklist and rubric first before working on the writing prompt.

Creating Checklists

When students approach a writing task, expectations should not be a mystery to them. It is incumbent on you to share the assessment criteria of a checklist and even a rubric so there is complete transparency in what students need to produce. When students know up front what is required, it helps shape their thinking and position them well to aim for a bull's-eye. Therefore, present criteria early in the unit so students are well aware of the assignment requirements and expectations and can maximize their chances of a successful product (see figure 4.2 for an example). Instead of you using the writing checklist or rubric after they have finished their drafts, students use the tool while they are writing.

A student writing checklist, particularly for major assignments, is replete with expectations. For you, the checklist functions as a commitment to teaching myriad skills. You can teach some items separately and others in combination with one another. However, a student's final written product should represent a culmination of the various skills on the checklist.

Each genre has certain elements that help writers focus their work and aid readers to elicit meaning from it. Therefore, for comprehensive writing pieces, design a checklist to convey expectations that incorporate the genre-specific characteristic elements and structures of a sound, well-developed piece. For example, when creating an argument checklist, include customized line items such as, *I acknowledge and address counterclaims*, and *Logical reasons connect to my thesis*. In addition, include those skills that contribute to strong writing in general, such as, *I vary my sentence structure*, and *I maintain a consistent point of view throughout my paper*. Preparing a checklist in advance ensures that you thoughtfully and deliberately account for differing standards. This way, you can avoid accidentally omitting necessary writing skills.

You can, however, invite students to co-construct a checklist. This may occur, for example, with shorter writing assignments or ongoing routine tasks throughout the year. To collaboratively produce a checklist, students can meet in groups or pairs to discuss and list expectations for a particular writing task. They can then share their items with the class, defend those that are essential, and work together to fashion appropriate checklists. For a comprehensive writing assignment, extend the activity slightly. To do so, prepare your checklist to be sure you include what is necessary. Once students share their lists to arrive at a class-generated brainstorm of the expected criteria, distribute your prepared checklist. Have them cross-reference the lists. Discuss any discrepancies, and determine if items need to be added to or deleted from your prepared checklist. This kind of activity is important whether or not students contribute to building a checklist because it gives students ownership of each item on it.

Essentially, the checklist is like a recipe that is propped up on the counter as you cook a dish. When someone has repeatedly made an entrée and is a more experienced cook, he or she might not need to use a recipe every step of the way. If the cook's vision of a successful dish and how to make it is clear in his mind, the recipe's support may taper off, or he might use an abbreviated recipe. Inexperienced or nascent cooks benefit from the guidance of a recipe to assure they successfully follow the steps to produce an optimal outcome. Until students are proficient writers who know every aspect of what makes a particular writing piece stellar, the writing checklist will serve them well. Hence, the detail you include is incumbent on your students' expertise; if they are more adept writers, you may not need the detail shown in figure 4.2. In fact, students may use a rubric in lieu of checklists to guide and self-assess their writing, or use them both as tools for improvement. After reading the next section on rubrics, you can determine how you want to use both criteria mechanisms during instruction.

Short Story Writing Checklist

Short story writing task: After reading *The Curious Incident of the Dog in the Night-Time* by Mark Haddon, write a short story from the perspective of an individual with a disability so readers get an inside impression of his or her thoughts, feelings, emotions, and struggles. Use this checklist to guide you while writing.

General

- ❒ My title is original or creative.
- ❒ I structure new paragraphs appropriately.
- ❒ I show awareness of task, purpose, and audience.

Story Elements and Narrative Techniques

- ❒ My beginning engages readers; a central conflict sets my story in motion.
- ❒ I introduce the narrator and characters and establish a point of view and setting.
- ❒ I sequence the events in a logical order. If I use multiple plotlines, flashbacks, or flash-forwards, readers can follow the story line.
- ❒ My dialogue is purposeful because it moves the plot forward by revealing feelings, interactions between characters, reactions to setting or events, and so forth.
- ❒ My story is well paced and developed.
- ❒ I build suspense to create tension that entices readers.
- ❒ My ending resolves the central conflict and answers questions readers might have.

Sentence Structure and Transitions

- ❒ My writing doesn't include run-on sentences or fragments.
- ❒ I include appropriate and varied transitions to connect sentences so my writing flows.
- ❒ I also use transitions to show sequence and connect paragraphs. (Example: *After Marshall awoke on the third day of exile, life didn't seem as daunting. Until then, the situation was insurmountable.*)
- ❒ I vary my sentence beginnings and use different sentence patterns for rhythm and stylistic effect.

Description

- ❒ I use precise words and phrases, figurative language, and vivid details to describe events, settings, and characters.
- ❒ I use strong verbs in dialogue tags along with descriptions of reactions, gestures, and movements only as needed, not overdone.
- ❒ I use dialect, as appropriate, to signify geographical regions, era, social status, and so on.

Voice

- ❒ My writing maintains a consistent first person point of view from the perspective of a character.
- ❒ I use tone appropriately to convey an attitude or perspective of a character. In doing so, I demonstrate awareness of the character and situations, interactions, motivations, and so forth that affect him or her.

Grammar and Conventions

- ❒ I have correct grammar and usage.
- ❒ I check mechanics for accuracy—spelling, punctuation, and capitalization.
- ❒ My paper is formatted correctly with proper margins, headings, and font style, color, and size. If I handwrite, it's legible.

Figure 4.2: Sample short story writing checklist.

Visit ***go.SolutionTree.com/literacy*** *for a free reproducible version of this figure.*

Here are several points to keep in mind when designing checklists and incorporating them into your instructional program.

- **Use your standards and KUDs:** Be sure the checklist specifies what students should know, understand, and do, so it includes learning outcomes.
- **Align the checklist with the rubric:** The checklist guides students as they write. You will use the rubric to score student work, and students can also use it to self-assess and for peer critique. These pieces must match because it is unfair to assess them on items you haven't communicated as expectations. The next section addresses rubrics.
- **Write the checklist in first person:** Since students use the checklist as they write, personalizing it in this way implies ownership. Also, use student-friendly language so it is accessible.
- **Use present-tense verbs:** Students use the checklist in real time as they write, not as an afterthought.
- **Organize related items under subheadings:** This way, the checklist is easy to use and doesn't appear too cumbersome. For example, you might use headings for *ideas and content*, *evidence and elaboration*, and *sentence structure*; use headings specific to a genre shown in the narrative checklist in figure 4.2 (page 55); consider additional headings itemized in the rubric section that follows; and so forth.
- **Focus on discrete items or a combination of items as the basis for a lesson:** Use the checklist along with associated guiding questions to set the purpose for learning. For instance, post and point to this guiding question: *How can I begin sentences in different ways?* Then conduct a formal lesson so students learn that they can start sentences with adverbs, prepositional phrases, dependent clauses, subjects, or other structures. Show how this variety contributes to sentence fluency.
- **Exclude items that students have already mastered:** If you have already taught certain skills or your students are advanced writers, you might omit some line items, such as, *I spell words correctly* or *I punctuate dialogue properly*. Some teachers, though, choose to keep general line items on the checklist as reminders of strong writing attributes.
- **Focus on the final goal:** Avoid inputting line items that involve strategies to get to the final product. Instead, concentrate on what students should demonstrate in the paper. For example, *I use resources to check spelling* is certainly an action you want students to take; however, it focuses on the strategy. *I spell words correctly* is preferable as a checklist item since it highlights the final goal, which is to see a paper void of misspelled words. Or *I use the steps in the writing process*. Yes, you will definitely teach the steps and give time for students to work on each, but the final paper will reflect the outgrowth of employing the process.
- **Keep items brief:** Students will be able to refer to a lesson's resources or handouts if they need a reminder about what something means; therefore, keep line items on a checklist as brief as possible. For example, *I use appropriate and varied transitional words and phrases* does not have to go into depth about the variety of options (transitions to show location, time, comparison, and so forth) because students can find that information from a previously distributed handout or a bookmarked link.
- **Distribute a copy of the checklist:** Since the checklist is used as a guide while writing, each student should keep a copy in his or her writing folder or have an electronic copy available for easy access.
- **Include the writing task at the top of the checklist:** Craft and include a clear and succinct writing prompt at the top so students are aware of their writing assignment. Additionally, include the directive that students use the checklist as a guide while writing. (Review figure 4.2.)
- **Make sure the checklist is genre-specific:** If you are instructing students to produce a comprehensive piece of writing, create a genre-specific checklist, as shown in figure 4.2. This

way, students have a thorough awareness of the requirements of the assignment.

- **Draw attention to the checklist and how it can be used:** If you merely distribute the checklist and expect all students to use it as it is intended, you might be disappointed. Therefore, realize this could occur and turn it into an instructional experience. To do so, ask students to brainstorm with a partner or small group items that qualify as criteria for a solid paper in a particular genre. Students share their lists so you can generate a class list. Together, collapse items, delete unnecessary ones, and add to the list. Then distribute your prepared checklist, ask students to compare the two, and then discuss what is missing on either list. You might find that your list is incomplete, so add items that the class feels are warranted. Conduct this activity near the beginning of your unit so they know in advance what is expected. However, avoid doing this activity on the first days when they are unaware of any of the elements specific to the genre. Brainstorming what would be expected in a genre-specific piece checks for student understanding early on and also helps them become aware of the future paper's expectations.

Creating Rubrics

Along with designing a checklist, create a rubric—or scoring guide—for assessing student work based on criteria aligned to learning outcomes. Teachers can use rubrics across content areas to assess many different types of performances (such as dance routines, speeches, or the operation of equipment) or products (such as essays, shop-class projects, and PowerPoint slides) to show evidence of learning. They are also an effective teaching tool. Susan Brookhart (2013) says of rubrics:

> Rubrics are important because they clarify for students the qualities their work should have. This point is often expressed in terms of students understanding the learning target and criteria for success. For this reason, rubrics help teachers teach, they help coordinate instruction and assessment, and they help students learn. (p. 11)

Rubric Components

Whereas checklists catalog a list of requirements, all rubrics share the following three common components.

1. **Scoring criteria:** These are the specific elements to assess, such as a thesis statement, transitions, point of view, and so forth. I prefer to group these together under an overarching category. For example, expectations for complete sentences, sentence beginnings, run-on sentences, and fragments can be organized under the heading *Sentence Structure.*
2. **Levels of performance:** You can represent levels of performance to indicate how well the student has performed numerically, such as on a six-, five-, four-, or three-point scale. Or you can differentiate levels by terms such as *advanced, proficient, developing, basic,* and *below basic* or *advanced, proficient, partially proficient,* and *novice.* Four- or five-point rubrics are common. Alternatively, you can use a combination of a number and term (*5 = advanced*), which are usually located at the top of the rubric. Avoid evaluative terms such as *outstanding, excellent, competent,* or *poor.* Assign scores in whole numbers (one per level) or half scores, if a student's proficiency is between two levels.
3. **Criteria descriptors:** A description accompanies each scoring criterion along a continuum of quality based on the levels of performance. You use these descriptors to assess students' work. If students use rubrics to self-assess, these descriptors enable them to recognize the desirable standard of work they must present and how they can improve.

Figure 4.3 (page 58) offers a sample analytic rubric of these components, which includes a humorous depiction of criteria descriptors for a superhero.

Susan Brookhart (2013) separates criteria descriptors into two categories: low- and high-inference descriptions. Those that are high-inference require the assessor to make a decision and draw a conclusion about how to interpret the description. Consider these cells in figure 4.3: "Is faster than a speeding bullet" and "Is stronger than a tornado." To assess, one would have to determine at what speed the bullet is flying through the air and then judge the speed of the runner and ascertain the strength of a tornado. The same logic applies to the scoring criteria of the row "Accepting Responsibility." The

Scoring Criteria	Levels of Performance: Advanced	Very Effective	Effective	Marginally Effective	Ineffective
Producing Quality Work	Leaps tall buildings in a single bound	Must take a running start to leap over tall buildings	Can only leap over short buildings or medium buildings (no spires)	Crashes into buildings when attempting to jump over them	Cannot recognize buildings at all, let alone jump them
Using Work Time Effectively	Is faster than a speeding bullet	Is as fast as a speeding bullet	Is not quite as fast as a speeding bullet	Is as fast as a slow bullet	Wounds self with bullets when attempting to shoot a gun
Accepting Responsibility	Is stronger than a locomotive	Is stronger than a tornado	Is stronger than a hurricane	Shoots the breeze	Is full of hot air
Displaying Job Knowledge	Walks on water consistently	Walks on water in emergencies	Washes with water	Drinks water	Has eyes that water
Communicating Effectively	Talks with God	Talks with employees	Talks to himself or herself	Argues with himself or herself	Loses arguments with himself or herself

(Cells: Criteria Descriptors)

Source: Adapted from Kadushin & Harkness, 2002.

Figure 4.3: Components of a rubric.

subjective nature of the descriptors makes them high-inference. Alternatively, those that are more concrete and seemingly objective—like "Has eyes that water" and "Drinks water"—are low-inference because we can observe eyes watering and water being consumed (although it could be argued that the amount of tears seeping from the eyes or the intake of water is arbitrary, as well).

In a rubric on writing, "Minimal punctuation errors" requires more inference than "Two or three punctuation errors." However, the latter example with quantitative descriptors that don't involve inference can be misleading. Consider a student who produces a stellar and sophisticated paper that is lengthier and more intellectually developed than another student's average paper that is short and lacks content. The former student has more grammar errors and spotty control over mechanics. Scoring them both on a quantitative scale for grammar and conventions when the length and idea development are disparate does not reflect accurate assessment. When creating or revising a rubric, heed Brookhart's (2013) wise advice:

> You will find that most descriptions you use will require some level of inference, even when they appear to be objective. . . . The important point here is that leaving descriptions open to professional judgment—to making some inferences—is better than locking things down with overly rigid descriptions. Don't be tempted to make everything so low-inference (for example, "three errors in grammar") that you don't leave room for good judgment. The role of the descriptions is interpreting the criteria along a continuum of quality. (pp. 32–33)

Since scoring writing is rather subjective, you can use adverbs, verbs, adjectives, and description within the text of the performance-level criteria to differentiate one level from another. Figure 4.4 illustrates some of the many ways you can show the gradation of proficiency with criteria descriptors. Accompany the rubric with anchor papers—samples of student writing that exemplify each performance level to concretize the criteria. These are discussed later in the chapter (page 70).

Types of Rubrics

There are two types of rubrics—*analytic* and *holistic*. Holistic rubrics group similar items together so assessors get an overall view of a category of criteria items. In analytic rubrics, each skill represents a dedicated criteria

Opposing Claim Option 1 for an Argument (Adverb Descriptors)	
4	Clearly and thoughtfully acknowledges and addresses opposing claims
3	Somewhat acknowledges and addresses opposing claims
2	Weakly acknowledges and addresses opposing claims
1	Makes no mention of opposing claims or minimally acknowledges there is an opposing claim without addressing it
Opposing Claim Option 2 for an Argument (Verb Descriptors)	
4	Explains and refutes a relevant opposing claim
3	Explains an opposing claim
2	Identifies an opposing claim
1	Refers to no opposing claims
Evidence for an Argument (Adjective Descriptors)	
4	Includes a range of convincing evidence (facts, data, examples, and anecdotes) with thorough and sophisticated elaboration
3	Includes sufficient evidence and clear elaboration
2	Uses weak evidence and minimal elaboration
1	Relies on basic and superficial facts with no elaboration
Setting for a Narrative (More Description)	
4	The settings are clear and sophisticated. The paper is replete with precise words and phrases and sensory language to convey more than one vivid setting.
3	The setting is clear. The paper has an adequate amount of precise words and phrases and sensory language to convey a vivid setting.
2	The setting may be somewhat unclear. The paper needs additional precise words and phrases and sensory detail to convey a vivid setting.
1	The setting is unclear or confusing. There is minimal or no use of precise words and phrases or sensory language.

Punctuation (Grammar and Conventions)		
Option 1:	Option 2:	Option 3:
• No errors	• Rarely has errors	• Minor errors or no errors
• Minimal errors	• Minor errors	• Some errors
• Some significant errors	• Some errors	• Many errors
• Errors hinder (or interfere with) understanding	• Several errors	• Serious errors; hinders reading

Figure 4.4: Variations of rubric criteria descriptors.

item. For example, a holistic rubric might include a broad entry about the use of proper writing conventions instead of specifying which particular convention is the focus (such as proper use of subject-verb agreement or quotation marks in dialogue). Usually, holistic-scoring systems are used with an on-demand prompt for a school, district, or state summative assessment. They are efficient and useful when scoring student products on a large scale and can even work well for some classroom assessments to determine how the class performs as a whole to inform instruction. Although these rubrics do reflect students' strengths and weaknesses, they often provide a single score without feedback to identify specific areas that need attention or demonstrate where a student shows mastery.

When creating writing units where students move through the steps of the writing process and produce a comprehensive product, an analytic rubric is most effective. It is more functional than a holistic rubric since it provides you and students—when they are taught how to use them—with concrete information about performance pertaining to specific skills. Furthermore, analytic rubrics are descriptive rather than evaluative, functioning as tools to explain students' levels of performance. They can boost student achievement by describing at what level they are performing and where they need improvement. This allows for transparency about how the students are doing so they can be advocates for their own learning.

See an example of an analytical argumentation rubric in figure 4.5. Notice that it isolates each criterion so you can look across a row and identify students' strengths and weaknesses easily. You can then make instructional decisions about which skills to focus on for reteaching or enriching individual students, small groups, or the whole class. The end of the table shows levels of performance in percentages (100, 90, 80, and so forth) corresponding to numbers on a four-point scale. For additional information on how to use these numbers in grading, see Grading on page 72.

When you write your analytic rubric, target a writing genre or type, as shown in figure 4.5, so that you create a *general* or *common rubric*—an assessment tool that can be used for a variety of tasks that share a common focus. This way, teachers and students can use the same rubric for different assignments and also track progress over time in mastering a particular genre. For example, in language arts, one teacher might assign an argumentation essay in which students take a stand about specific merits that make a book or movie version of a literary work more compelling. Another instructor asks students to identify the most prominent theme in a complex text and defend it. A history teacher might ask students to convince readers of the most effective qualities all political leaders must possess. Another might assign students to write an argument in response to the question, *Should the government allow immigrants who are in the United States illegally to become citizens?* In science, one class writes an essay for or against the debate about whether human activity is responsible for global climate change. Students in another class can each choose his or her own debatable science topic concerning the environment, such as fossil fuels versus nuclear energy or oil drilling in the Arctic regions. Although the tasks vary, all teachers and students utilize the same analytic general or common rubric—in this example, an argumentation rubric—to assess work.

Guidelines for Rubric Design

Following are guidelines and suggestions for designing or redesigning a rubric for a culminating assessment.

- **Include scoring criteria that target knowledge or skills (like the thesis statement, evidence, or elaboration):** The criteria should characterize evidence of student learning based on standards and learning goals. You can group these elements under overarching categories. For example, the 6+1 Trait Writing model of instruction and assessment from the Northwest Regional Educational Laboratory (http://educationnorthwest.org/traits/traits-rubrics) uses the following categories, or traits, in their rubrics: ideas, organization, voice, word choice, sentence fluency, conventions, and presentation. Under each are specific criteria items. For example, the organization trait includes lead, conclusion, transitions, sequencing, text structure, and more. Besides these overarching categories, you might include the following.
    - Statement of purpose
    - Development of ideas
    - Content
    - Focus
    - Story elements and narrative techniques
    - Argumentation support and elaboration
    - Use of sources (or research)

Directions: Score the paper by circling the appropriate rubric scale score for each criteria item. To arrive at a single score, determine the mode or median based on all the scores. For items that are weighted double, input the score twice in your calculations. Then use the conversion scale at the end of this figure to arrive at a percentage score and translate to a grade, if needed.

IDEA AND DEVELOPMENT

Criteria	4.0 – 3.5	3.0 – 2.5	2.0 – 1.5	1.0 – 0.5	0.0
Task, Purpose, and Audience Adhere to the task, purpose, and audience.	*Clear focus on the task and purpose that takes into account the needs of the audience*	*Clear focus on the task and articulates the purpose*	*Generally articulates the topic in task*	*Unaware of task, purpose, and audience*	
	4.0 3.5	3.0 2.5	2.0 1.5	1.0 0.5	0.0
Title Include a distinctive or original title to support the topic.	*Conveys claim in a distinctive and compelling way; sophisticated*	*Conveys claim in an original way*	*Conveys claim in a straightforward way*	*Confusing tie to claim*	*No title*
	4.0 3.5	3.0 2.5	2.0 1.5	1.0 0.5	0.0
Introduction: Hook and Context Create a hook to draw in the reader and provide context.	*Attractive opening draws in readers and provides clear context for argument; sophisticated*	*Opening draws in readers and provides context*	*Opening attempts to engage and provides some context*	*Weakly stated hook or insufficient context; clearly incomplete*	*No hook or context*
	4.0 3.5	3.0 2.5	2.0 1.5	1.0 0.5	0.0
Introduction: Thesis Introduce a claim through the thesis statement; use a subordinate clause to set up the argument; focus on debatable topic.	*Thoughtful thesis clearly states the claim and includes a subordinate clause to set up the argument; focuses on debatable topic; sophisticated*	*Thesis states claim using subordinate clause as setup; focuses on debatable topic*	*Thesis focuses on debatable topic*	*Weakly stated or unclear thesis; not debatable*	*No thesis*
	4.0 3.5	3.0 2.5	2.0 1.5	1.0 0.5	0.0

Figure 4.5: Argumentation writing rubric.

continued ➤

IDEA AND DEVELOPMENT

Criterion	4.0–3.5	3.0–2.5	2.0–1.5	1.0–0.5	0.0
Body Paragraphs: Reasoning Support the claim with logical reasons.	*Clear, logical, and compelling reasons link tightly to thesis; logically ordered to enhance argument; sophisticated*	*Clear and logical reasons support the thesis; logically ordered*	*Reasons sometimes provide loose connections to thesis or general topic; order somewhat haphazard in places*	*Weak, illogical, or incomplete reasons; lacks connection to thesis*	
	4.0 3.5	3.0 2.5	2.0 1.5	1.0 0.5	0.0
Body Paragraphs: Evidence Use relevant evidence from multiple accurate, credible sources; integrate evidence smoothly; use no plagiarizing; include proper citation.	*Altogether relevant, accurate, compelling, and developed evidence (facts, data, examples) from multiple credible sources to support claim; seamless integration; proper citations throughout; sophisticated*	*Relevant, accurate, and developed evidence (facts, data, examples) from multiple credible sources to support claim; smooth integration; proper citations*	*Relevant evidence; limited credible sources used; evidence somewhat developed to support claim; choppy integration; most citations included*	*Any of these apply: little, if any, evidence to support position; irrelevant evidence; lacks development; one source used; mostly incorrect or plagiarized; lacks complete citations*	
	4.0 3.5	3.0 2.5	2.0 1.5	1.0 0.5	0.0
Body Paragraphs: Elaboration and Ending Interpret, explain, or provide commentary of the evidence; provide a paragraph conclusion.	*Elaboration provides clear and astute interpretation of necessary evidence; concluding sentence wraps up paragraph well or segues to next one*	*Strong elaboration provided most of the time to interpret evidence; satisfying ending sentence*	*Some elaboration provided; ending somewhat satisfying*	*Weak, incorrect, or missing elaboration; weak ending sentence*	*No elaboration and ending sentence*
	4.0 3.5	3.0 2.5	2.0 1.5	1.0 0.5	0.0

	Criteria	4.0 – 3.5	3.0 – 2.5	2.0 – 1.5	1.0 – 0.5	0.0
IDEA AND DEVELOPMENT	**Counterclaims** Acknowledge alternate or opposing claims and distinguish the claim(s) from the asserted position by providing counterevidence and elaboration.	*Clearly and thoughtfully acknowledges and refutes the opposing claim(s); well structured in either its own paragraph of woven throughout paper; sophisticated*	*Acknowledges and addresses opposing claim(s); clear structure within paper*	*Somewhat acknowledges and addresses opposing claim(s); structure somewhat intact*	*Weakly acknowledges opposing claim(s); haphazard structure*	*No acknowl-edgment of opposing claim*
IDEA AND DEVELOPMENT	**Conclusion** Provide a concluding statement or section that follows from and supports the argument presented.	*Clearly sums up thesis and important points without repeating verbatim; call to action (if needed) or reflective ending clearly strong; sophisticated*	*Sums up thesis and important points fairly well; no repetition of thesis; call to action (if needed) or reflective ending strong*	*Adequately sums up thesis and important points; little or no repetition of thesis; call to action (if needed) or reflective ending somewhat strong*	*Weakly sums up thesis or important points or repeats thesis almost or entirely verbatim; incomplete; weak or no call to action (if needed) or reflective ending*	*No conclusion*
ORGANIZATION	**Structure** Organize body paragraphs and evidence within them logically to facilitate a convincing argument.	*Logically organized as a whole paper and within paragraphs to facilitate comprehension in support of a position; sophisticated*	*Mostly logically organized*	*Somewhat logically organized*	*Weak or haphazard organization; difficult to follow*	
ORGANIZATION	**Paragraphing** Know when to begin a new paragraph and how to indent paragraphs.	*Paragraphing and indenting completely intact*	*Mostly all correct usage of paragraphing and indenting*	*Some paragraphing errors*	*Mostly all one paragraph*	*Multiple-paragraph paper reduced to one paragraph*

continued ➤

Category	Criterion	4.0–3.5	3.0–2.5	2.0–1.5	1.0–0.5	0.0
LANGUAGE AND STYLE	**Point of View / Style** Maintain consistent point of view; establish and maintain formal style and objective tone.	*Maintains consistent point of view throughout paper; consistently uses formal style and objective tone suited to audience; sophisticated*	*Mostly consistent point of view; generally uses formal style and objective tone*	*Point of view somewhat intact; adequately uses formal style and objective tone*	*Weak sense of point of view; style and tone inconsistent; informal style and subjective tone*	
		4.0 3.5	3.0 2.5	2.0 1.5	1.0 0.5	0.0
	Word Choice Use grade-appropriate general academic and domain-specific words and phrases; select and use strong words appropriate for an argument (i.e., pointed yet not biased or emotional); avoid unnecessary repetition.	*Consistently accurate and strong choice and usage of words and phrases; sophisticated language; no emotionally charged words or repetition (unless used for effect)*	*Mostly accurate and strong choice and usage of words and phrases; no emotional or biased language; some unnecessary repetition, but minor*	*Adequate choice and usage of words and phrases; some emotionally charged or biased language; fair amount of unnecessary repetition*	*Rarely uses appropriate or strong words and phrases; emotionally charged language; replete with unnecessary repetition*	
		4.0 3.5	3.0 2.5	2.0 1.5	1.0 0.5	0.0
TRANSITIONS AND SENTENCE STRUCTURE	**Transitions From Paragraph to Paragraph** Use words, phrases, and clauses between paragraphs to create cohesion and clarify the relationships among claim, counterclaims, reasons, and evidence.	*Thoughtful use of transitions to link paragraphs and create cohesion and clarification; sophisticated*	*Appropriate and sufficient transitions used to link paragraphs and create cohesion and clarification*	*Somewhat appropriate and sufficient transitions used*	*Weak use of transitions; additional or more appropriate transitions needed*	*No transitions to link para-graphs*
		4.0 3.5	3.0 2.5	2.0 1.5	1.0 0.5	0.0
	Transitions Between Sentences Use transitions within paragraphs for fluid reading.	*Thoughtful use of transitional words, phrases, and clauses to link sentences; very fluid reading; sophisticated*	*Appropriate and sufficient transitions to connect sentences so reading flows*	*Somewhat appropriate and sufficient use of transitions*	*Little or no transitions within paragraph; very halted reading*	*No transitions to link sentences*
		4.0 3.5	3.0 2.5	2.0 1.5	1.0 0.5	0.0

Category	Criterion	4.0–3.5	3.0–2.5	2.0–1.5	1.0–0.5	0.0
TRANSITIONS AND SENTENCE STRUCTURE	**Complete Sentences** Produce complete sentences; no run-ons.	*No run-ons; all sentences are complete*	*Minimal sentence structure errors*	*Sentence structure errors sometimes distract from reading*	*Many sentence structure errors interfere with meaning*	
		4.0 3.5	3.0 2.5	2.0 1.5	1.0 0.5	0.0
	Sentence Beginning Variety Include a variety of sentence beginnings.	*Thoughtful, consistent, and sophisticated use of a variety of sentence beginnings (for example, subjects, prepositional phrases, adverbs, and dependent clauses)*	*Variety of sentence beginnings used*	*Some sentences begin in the same way*	*Most or all sentences begin in the same way by either the same word or the same type (e.g., all subjects)*	
		4.0 3.5	3.0 2.5	2.0 1.5	1.0 0.5	0.0
	Sentence Structure Variety Vary sentence patterns for meaning and style (for example, simple, compound, complex).	*Thoughtful, consistent, and sophisticated use of sentence structure variety*	*Mostly uses sentence structure variety*	*Most sentences have the same sentence structure, so there is little cadence*	*All sentences are simple and/or compound*	
		4.0 3.5	3.0 2.5	2.0 1.5	1.0 0.5	0.0
FORMAT, GRAMMAR, CONVENTIONS	**Presentation and Formatting** Adhere to proper formatting for a paper, in-text citations, and a Works Cited document.	*Completely adheres to proper formatting*	*Mostly adheres to proper formatting*	*Somewhat adheres to proper formatting*	*Altogether weak formatting that confuses and distracts readers*	*No format*
		4.0 3.5	3.0 2.5	2.0 1.5	1.0 0.5	0.0
	Grammar Use proper grammar, including writing in active voice and using correct verb tense.	*Minimal or no errors*	*Minor errors*	*Some errors*	*Serious errors; hinders reading*	
		4.0 3.5	3.0 2.5	2.0 1.5	1.0 0.5	0.0

continued ➤

FORMAT, GRAMMAR, CONVENTIONS

Criterion	Minimal or no errors	Minor errors	Some errors	Serious errors; hinders reading	
Capitalization Use correct capitalization.	4.0 3.5	3.0 2.5	2.0 1.5	1.0 0.5	0.0
Punctuation Punctuate correctly, including quoted material and in-text citations.	4.0 3.5	3.0 2.5	2.0 1.5	1.0 0.5	0.0
Spelling Spell correctly.	4.0 3.5	3.0 2.5	2.0 1.5	1.0 0.5	0.0

After determining the mode or median, identify the corresponding percentage and issue a grade based on your preferred scale of what constitutes an A, A–, B+, and so forth.

Percentage	100	95	90	85	80	75	70	65	60
Rubric	4.0	3.5	3.0	2.5	2.0	1.5	1.0	0.5	0.0

Source: Kathy Tuchman Glass and Nicole Dimich Vagle.

Visit ***go.SolutionTree.com/literacy*** *for a free reproducible version of this figure.*

- Language
- Language and style
- Tone and style
- Vocabulary
- Description
- Organizational structure or text structure
- Transitions and sentence structure
- Grammar usage and conventions (or mechanics)
- Format (or presentation)
- Text features

- **Write descriptors for what is being assessed on a continuum of quality:** Aim for clear language, although realize that some descriptors will be subjective. It is incumbent upon the assessor to use professional expertise along with anchor papers to determine scores of most criteria items.
- **Find and use anchor papers for scoring purposes and within instruction:** Since there is some subjectivity when scoring, identify anchor papers to accompany a rubric. These papers can serve as instructional tools within a lesson when leading students in an exercise to critique and score them. They can also educate parents or guardians about tangible examples of performance. Additionally, anchor papers serve as benchmarks for scoring since they represent a standard against which to assess other papers. To issue reliable scores, collaborate with colleagues in calibration sessions to collect anchor papers so there is scoring consistency. (For more information, see Identifying Anchor Papers and Calibration on page 70.)
- **Avoid quantitative descriptors:** Rather than using numbers, such as *one to two grammar errors, two to four similes or metaphors,* or *five to seven examples of figurative language,* keep your descriptors more open ended: for

example, *minor errors*, *some errors*, or *replete with errors*; or *uses a variety of introspective figurative language that adds dimension and fresh perspective*, *uses figurative language that enhances text in some places*, or *uses simplistic figurative language*. This way, students with longer papers who have more grammar errors are not penalized unfairly or those who write more sophisticated examples of figurative language are given due credit and measured qualitatively. This method allows for more leeway in scoring and applying sound judgment.

- **Avoid redundancy and overlap:** Make each item dedicated to a specific criterion. If two cells are very similar or overlap, writing can be hard to score, and students may be unfairly penalized twice.
- **Use a consistent performance-level scale across your school and even district:** It's confusing for students if one teacher scores on a five-point scale and another on a four-point scale. Depending on the content area, the criteria will naturally vary, but if the point system is familiar to students, it will help them understand the values associated with different criteria items. Consider conferring with colleagues to support this suggestion.
- **Weight scores, as appropriate:** Not every item needs to have the same scoring structure. Consider double-weighting significant aspects of writing content, such as big-ticket ones like reasoning, evidence, and elaboration, or descriptive setting, purposeful dialogue, and suspense. Furthermore, sometimes a zero works for an item if there's an instance where it is nonexistent in the paper, such as a title or paragraphing. For grading suggestions, see Grading on page 72.
- **Invite students to contribute to rubric design:** Although it is important that you are well aware of what constitutes levels of performance and the criteria to score (based on standards and your professional expertise), allow opportunities for students to co-construct or review your prepared rubric. When they suggest changes, though, ask them to provide evidence from student or published work that supports their reasons for the addition, deletion, or revision.

Rubrics as an Instructional Tool

Since both the checklist and analytic rubric should align to standards and learning outcomes, they complement one another and can both be useful tools throughout the writing process to improve student proficiency. The rubric can serve many functions—as a self- and peer-assessment tool, and also for you to score the student's final product. Be sure to present it early in the unit so expectations and tools for scoring students' papers are clearly articulated. Try out the following ideas.

- **Orient students to the format of the rubric to familiarize them with its structure:** Explain the parts of the rubric—scoring criteria, levels of performance, and criteria descriptors. Model how to use it to score an assignment using anonymous sample student work.
- **Create a student-friendly rubric, if the language is too advanced:** Alternatively, give students resources so they can translate the rubric with a partner or small group if the language is cumbersome to them. Then, have them share their translations with the class to compare findings. You can do this in segments so students do not tackle the entire rubric at once.
- **Concentrate on one line item or section of the rubric at a time:** Teach a targeted skill or related skills reflected in a line or section of the rubric. After instruction, have students self-assess or critique each other's papers based on the focus of the learning experience.
- **Have students self-assess at different places in the writing process:** They can score their work after the first draft, receive feedback from peers, revise to generate another draft, and then self-assess again using the rubric to chart their improvement and inform their next steps.
- **Score papers by matching criteria with examples:** For self-assessment or peer review, students can score the paper using a different colored highlighter for different categories of the rubric and use corresponding colors to

indicate areas in their paper that match. For example, all scores associated with sentence fluency may be highlighted in blue on the rubric, and instances in the paper where this is evident are also highlighted blue. Using the rubric formatively in this way invites opportunities for revision.

Utilizing Student Writing Models

Along with checklists and rubrics, a third mechanism that can assist students in producing high-quality culminating assessments is examining the work of others. When learning something new, we typically study someone else's work to help guide us. We notice and analyze the form, technique, and end product so we can imitate it. This is true of mastering a tennis swing, preparing a soufflé, or learning a new dance. Oftentimes, we review the example or a live or recorded demonstration repeatedly until we feel ready to embark on the task ourselves. We can look at the whole picture and then break it into parts to tease out the skills required to be successful. This same concept applies to writing.

As well as using texts from published authors, it is prudent to use student writing models as an instructional tool to examine whole papers and also home in on specific criteria items (such as use of transitions or thesis construction). Therefore, provide opportunities for students to assess published and student writing samples against the criteria. Conduct lessons in which they examine, analyze, and discuss the strengths and weaknesses of specific characteristics and structure related to a genre and also elements of strong writing in general against the criteria. For example, use writing models of an argumentation essay to help students identify poor and weak examples of integrating evidence, citing sources, or staking a claim through a thesis. Ask them to critique the level of suspense in a narrative to determine if it creates the right amount of tension or falls short. Or have them study an informational report to determine if text features enhance or detract from the topic or if the writer needs to supplement subheadings, graphics, or other features. Additionally, instruct them to assess treatment of general writing techniques, such as appropriate uses of transitions, consistent point of view, and so forth.

Feature poor and mediocre as well as stellar samples. Orchestrate situations in which students examine and study them side by side. This practice of juxtaposing different samples with varying degrees of proficiency in particular areas of writing will help students recognize the presence or absence of certain attributes. As a consequence, it will strengthen their writing skills as they emulate and apply what they learn in their own work. Plus, they learn how to give salient feedback to others to contribute to peers' writing performance.

Carefully select appropriate writing samples that target skills as the basis for a lesson. In terms of featuring writing samples from students in your own classroom, use caution. Sometimes peers hesitate to provide honest feedback for fear of hurting their classmates' feelings. Other times, it can swing in the opposite direction, and students can be harsh. It is typically safer to use anonymous examples from a different class or prior years or find unknown papers from print or online sources.

Resources for Student Writing Models

Peruse websites, your own resources, or any anchor papers you already have to search for writing models. The examples from the following websites vary in quality, grade level, and writing type or genre. Some papers provide annotations; however, use your own professional judgment and expertise to determine whether you agree with the comments. Consider asking students to compare their impressions with reviewers' as an instructional exercise. Additionally, consider your grade level and subject matter as you select papers, but don't feel relegated to using examples from only the grade level you teach. Perhaps papers in the grade below or above might serve you well in teaching to a particular point. Visit the following websites for resources, or visit **go.SolutionTree.com/literacy** to access materials related to this book.

- **Achieve the Core** (http://achievethecore.org/category/330/student-writing-samples)
- **"Appendix C: Samples of Student Writing" of the Common Core State Standards** (www.corestandards.org/assets/Appendix_C.pdf)
- **Brown's Student Learning Tools** (www.mesacc.edu/~paoih30491/StudentLearningTools.html)
- **Holt, Rinehart and Winston Writing Prompts** (http://my.hrw.com/support/hos/host_models_list_Fall_2006.html)

- **Literacy Design Collaborative's Student Work Samples** (https://ldc.org/resources#Student-Work-Samples)
- **Oregon Department of Education** (www.ode.state.or.us/search/page/?=527)
- **Oregon State University's Sample Essays** (http://people.oregonstate.edu/~petersp/ORST/WR121_files/argument.htm#Sample%20Essays)
- **Thoughtful Learning Student Models** (https://k12.thoughtfullearning.com/resources/studentmodels)

Instructional Strategy Suggestions for Using Student and Published Examples

There are various strategies to employ when asking students to critique student or published models. Following are ideas to consider as the basis for a lesson. Students can work in pairs or small groups and then report out to the whole class, as appropriate. Alternatively, (1) they can first work independently and then confer with group members, or (2) small groups can work on an activity and then share and discuss their work with another small group or the class. Strategically select the student model or published sample (see Complex Texts in the appendix of this book) that aligns with your lesson focus.

- **Identify text structure:** In this exercise, students read strong samples and complete a graphic organizer based on the structure and content of the piece. Alternatively, they may create their own organizer on a blank screen or paper or use an electronic tool or app. If students design the organizer, it becomes a dual exercise in which they must first determine the structure that aligns with the author's purpose so they can create an appropriate graphic organizer (for example, cause and effect, sequential, comparison and contrast) and then input content. To differentiate, assign students different texts to use as the basis for their work. Assign or allow them to choose a graphic organizer rather than assuming that only one type will be appropriately challenging or appeal to all students' learning styles in your class.

  For struggling learners, prepare a partially completed graphic organizer for a preselected writing sample. Once students complete their organizers, discuss how the writing is structured, and highlight other elements that contribute to attributes of a featured genre. Here are links to various graphic organizers.

  - edHelper.com (www.edhelper.com/teachers/graphic_organizers.htm)
  - Education Oasis (http://educationoasis.com/curriculum/graphic_organizers.htm)
  - Freeology (http://freeology.com/graphicorgs)
  - Houghton Mifflin Harcourt Education Place (www.eduplace.com/graphicorganizer)
  - Teacher Files (www.teacherfiles.com/resources_organizers.htm)
  - TeacherVision (www.teachervision.com/graphic-organizers/printable/6293.html)
- **Notice when a paper is underdeveloped:** Conduct a similar exercise to the previous bullet, but this time, select mediocre student samples as the basis for completing a graphic organizer. Your aim is for the students to realize papers are incomplete, which ostensibly happens when they cannot finish the entire graphic organizer. Have them suggest ways that the writer could add information. Students can even revise the written work and compare what they added to make the writing more developed. Additionally, you can conduct the exercise that follows, where students identify elements and study content with weak papers as another way to notice when work is inferior and what makes it so.
- **Identify genre elements and assess the content:** This is a two-step exercise conducted with strong student and published samples. It provides students the opportunity to carefully examine what contributes to fine writing. First, instruct students to label parts of a paper in any one of the ways in the following list to focus on the characteristic elements of a genre.

- Students use a highlighter to color-code elements of the paper. Ask students to provide a key to identify colors that correspond to each text element (such as yellow for factual evidence and green for reasons and topic sentences).
- Provide students with sticky notes to affix to the paper, and have them label the text excerpt with the relevant element.
- Prepare small card labels with parts of the paper written on each one, such as *thesis*, *reason*, *fact*, *data*, and *opposing claim*. Have students place each label next to the part of the paper.
- Have students write the text element in the margin and underline or highlight the corresponding text excerpt.

Second, facilitate discussions in which students study the writer's craft, noticing the actual content and not just the presence of an element. Besides using the rubric to validate that these samples are exemplary, focus on having students find evidence to support their assertions. They can discuss their reactions, interpretations, impressions, analogies, and connections that emanate from excellent writing.

- **Compare and contrast genre elements:** The previous activity asks for students to focus on one writing genre and identify its elements. You might have differentiated by instructing students to read different writing samples, but they all shared common elements since they were the same genre or text type. In this exercise, purposely assign small groups a different genre or text type, and ask them to perform one of the labeling choices in the previous bullet. Groups then compare their work and discuss the attributes specific to each writing sample. Comparing and contrasting characteristic elements and structure can reinforce the type or specific genre of writing as the focus for your current unit, review past learning, and preview genres in upcoming units of instruction.
- **Critique annotations:** Find appropriate examples that include annotations (see Resources for Student Writing Models, page 68). Ask students to read the papers and corresponding annotations and then write responses or orally discuss the reviewers' annotations. In doing so, they state whether they agree or disagree and provide evidence from the student work to support their impressions. Students can work in homogeneous groups and read text at the right challenge levels. Or they can work in heterogeneous groups and read text based on topics that interest them.
- **Assess student samples:** Teach students how to use a rubric to score sample papers. Model how to do this using the think-aloud strategy to articulate out loud your thinking as you score one item at a time. When modeling, invite students to participate and share their rationale for how they might assign scores based on the performance levels in the rubric. Then ask students to score samples in pairs and share their impressions with another partnership and confer. If any group has a discrepancy in scoring, ask them to share with the whole class for a discussion. When teaching students to assess writing, use all levels of student work so they have authentic practice that they can apply to their own papers and offer advice to others. In short, do not focus exclusively on exemplary samples, as there is intrinsic value in seeing where writing falls short and how it can be fixed. Also see the activity on page 67, Score papers by matching criteria with examples.

Identifying Anchor Papers and Calibration

It's advisable to identify anchor papers to be proactive in your teaching. For one, you'll conduct lessons around writing samples like those explained previously and throughout the book. You can organize these papers by genre and then more specifically by skills within that genre. Having an inventory of papers categorized by levels of performance for these genres, skills, and papers as a whole will focus teaching and learning. For instance, create paper or electronic folders for a narrative unit. One can house masterful dialogue examples of how this literary device moves the plot forward in an intentional way along with other writing that shows superfluous, meaningless dialogue that needs rewriting. Another folder can house those illustrative of a sound, well-developed piece with grammar and conventions intact to show an entirely strong narrative.

Besides finding appropriate papers for teaching purposes, you'll also need anchor papers to guide you in grading students' work. To do so, conduct calibration sessions with colleagues to take advantage of their expertise and input to determine if there is consistency in interpreting each level of the rubric. In these sessions, together you'll calibrate—or come to an agreement or common understanding about—examples of proficiency levels in response to the same assessment using the same rubric. Participating in a calibration session with colleagues who are invested in the same or a similar assignment and rubric prepares you to score your own students' papers independently with more confidence and reliability (SCALE, 2015). If you are the only teacher of a grade level in your school, solicit a colleague in the grade above or below yours to score with you. You could also orchestrate an online session with other teaching peers through Google Hangouts or Skype to examine and discuss student work.

Calibrating to score papers helps ensure that you and your colleagues apply the rubric uniformly. Together, you'll discuss differences in how to interpret high-inference items using student examples as evidence and work toward building consensus. During conversations, you'll suggest changes that need to be made to the prompt or rubric. If there are criteria items that are still in dispute, then "improve the clarity of the rubric so that the teachers agree more easily on what the score of a piece of student work will be" (Reeves, 2016, p. 94).

At this type of meeting, each teacher should come prepared with representative sample work—high-, medium-, and low-scoring papers—to use as the basis for discussion and calibration. Be sure to schedule a session with colleagues early during the teaching of your unit so that when students turn in their papers, you can give them timely feedback on their scores. The goal is to leave with agreed-upon student or sample work to use as anchor papers across performance levels. As stated, you'll use them when independently scoring your own students' work and also within your classroom for instructional purposes. You can even share these papers during parent conferences so family members and guardians are aware of how to interpret rubric scores. Since you are just designing this unit and haven't piloted it yet, you do not have the advantage of anchor papers for this particular writing assignment. You could, though, find similar papers from the student model resources offered in this book. Next year, you can use papers from this current school year as your anchors.

For additional information on calibration protocol and details about how to lead sessions, peruse these resources. Visit **go.SolutionTree.com/literacy** to access the free reproducibles. Additional ways to use anchor papers while piloting a unit are discussed in chapter 6 (page 90).

- "Writing Calibration Protocol" (Rhode Island Department of Education, 2013; www.ride.ri.gov/Portals/0/Uploads/Documents/Common-Core/RIDE_Calibration_Process.pdf)
- "Calibration Protocol for Scoring Student Work: A Part of the Assessment Toolkit" (Rhode Island Department of Education; www.ride.ri.gov/Portals/0/Uploads/Documents/Teachers-and-Administrators-Excellent-Educators/Educator-Evaluation/Online-Modules/Calibration_Protocol_for_Scoring_Student_Work.pdf)
- "Semi-Structured Calibration Activity" (SCALE, n.d.; http://performanceassessmentresourcebank.org/system/files/SCALE%20Semi-Structured%20Calibration%20Activity%20Protocol.pdf)
- *FAST Grading: A Guide to Implementing Best Practices* (Reeves, 2016)

During calibration, you and your colleagues will engage in honest discussion and respectful debates about student performance and evidence to support impressions based on the rubric. Before beginning, have a conversation about the potential hazards of scoring bias. Teachers sometimes unknowingly adopt a biased view when reading a student's paper, which can impact the score. To become aware of this tendency, review the following common forms of scorer bias (Spandel, 2001).

- **The look of the paper:** Papers that are illegible or messy, have stilted handwriting, or are void of margins or paragraph breaks fall prey to bias. By the same token, papers that are neat and long can mistakenly be scored favorably, the scorer thinking these features equate with stronger content than the paper is worth.

- **Personal beliefs:** Sometimes a scorer has difficulty separating his or her beliefs from that of the writer. This can happen particularly with argumentation essays or even personal narratives where controversial or sensitive issues are the focus. Either they can swing compassionately or harshly, letting their personal views bias the score.
- **Pet peeves:** Some scorers are sticklers for particular aspects of a paper and weigh these favored criteria items more heavily. Grammar and conventions are often the culprits, as scorers rely too much on the absence or presence of these writing features.
- **The human factor:** Sometimes teachers score liberally because they sense the student makes a strong effort but misses the mark; therefore, they issue a sympathy score. Other times, they are just plain tired, and natural fatigue skews the scoring inadvertently. Then there are those who can't help but score too harshly or lightly. Their personality gets in the way, and they translate how they view the world. (Think of glass-half-empty or -full kind of people.) And still, there are some who are offended by profanity, which can interfere with objectivity.

Rubrics can help avoid reviewer bias by eliminating such items from the scoring criteria. Attention is instead focused on the ideas and contents of the paper, allowing for more unbiased grading.

Grading

Students produce all sorts of work throughout the writing process—graphic organizers, notes from research, drafts of setting descriptions for a narrative, lists of words they might want to use, and so forth. Do not feel compelled to grade each and every piece of work that students submit during the writing process—giving feedback, yes; grading, not always. Alfie Kohn (2006, as cited in Hattie, 2012) says, "Never mark students while they are still learning" (p. 152). To this, Hattie (2012) adds:

> Students see the mark, so often, as the "end" of the learning. . . . The comments can provide justification for the grade, but there is little evidence that the comments lead to changes in student learning behaviours, or greater effort, or more deliberate practice—mainly because students see the "work" as finished. (p. 152)

When students submit their finished writing assignment, you'll use the rubric to score the work. You can attach the rubric to the paper and circle or highlight descriptors on the rubric that signify their performance level. It is unnecessary to write extensive comments since the descriptors provide some clarity about where students stand against a criteria item, which is a convenient time saver and reduces time spent commenting at length. I remember well scoring 160 papers repeatedly throughout a school year! Although I conveyed most feedback via the rubric, I would add a general comment to accompany what I highlighted in the rubric to emphasize something that stood out, such as, "You have mastered the art of sentence fluency! I notice how there is a nice rhythm to your writing." Or, "It's clear you grasp figurative language. I particularly like your simile: 'His aura transfixed us like mesmerized robots as we followed him to the abandoned farmhouse.'" Or, "You chose a tough topic for your essay, and I'm impressed by your thoughtful and logical reasons to support your position." I might follow an encouraging comment with a future goal, such as, "Now that you've masterfully grasped sentence fluency, next time I suggest you focus on using more imagery to describe a setting."

Since you're conducting a unit around a curriculum-embedded performance assessment, where the process and product ensure you have infused safeguards, scaffolds, and support during instructional experiences throughout the unit, there should not be many low rubric scores. But what if some students' scores are subpar? Once students submit their papers, it needn't be the end of the line. That is more indicative of a summative assessment, in which you record the grade in the gradebook and march on. Rather, if we want to produce strong writers with a commitment to continual improvement, offer students the opportunity to return to their papers and revise them at a later time. After all, our overriding goal is for students to acquire new skills and strategies and then take what they learn and apply it over and over again until it's intuitive. In fact, writing teacher and author Penny Kittle (2008) put this into practice when she announced to her students:

> I have a proposal. I care *most* that you write well, not *when* you write well, so you may continue to revise a piece of writing all semester. There is no last draft until you say so. The final grade for a unit will be on your best draft, even if it is months after our initial deadline. (p. 222)

She told her students that sometimes when they submit a paper within the deadline, it may not be representative of their best work, and she wanted to grant them time to improve it. She made it clear, however, that this option was not about procrastination. If students failed to work hard and to write in the allotted time frame, the offer was off the table. Although it would seem unwieldy to grade again the onslaught of papers that might follow after already having graded them, she reports that it was not as you would imagine:

> This did not result in a lot of extra grading as I feared, but it has produced some truly fine pieces of writing as well as students who realize all they're capable of when they set aside excuses and keep at it. (Kittle, 2008, p. 223)

I say, it's worth a try in the interest of your valuable charges.

Translating rubric scores to a letter grade can be tricky because they are two different scoring systems. Rubrics provide detailed information about how students perform against a host of criteria items; hence, they uncover areas needing improvement and reveal what has been mastered. The reality in a classroom is that oftentimes, teachers need to issue a grade for the writing piece. Susan Brookhart (2013) offers direction for how to do this: "If you do need one overall grade . . . and must summarize an assessment with one overall score, use the median *or* mode, *not* the mean, of the scores for each criterion" (p. 114).

To determine a score or letter grade, use or create a rubric like the one for argumentation in figure 4.5 (beginning on page 61). Score each student's paper by circling the appropriate rubric scale score for each criteria item—title, thesis, counterclaims, structure, and so on. Apply one of the methods illustrated in table 4.1 to determine the mode or median based on all the scores. If

Table 4.1: Determining Median and Mode

For illustrative purposes, a student earns these scores on eleven criteria items on a 4-point scale:
1, 2, 2, 2, 3, 3, 3, 3, 4, 4, 4.
Here is how to calculate the median and mode.

Definition	How to Do It	Example
Median The middle value of a set of numbers	• Rewrite the list of numbers in order from smallest to largest. • Select the middle one. • If there is an odd number of items, the median is the middle entry after sorting the numbers in order. • If the list of numbers is even, calculate the median by adding the two middle numbers and dividing by two.	1, 2, 2, 2, 3, (3,) 3, 3, 4, 4, 4
Mode The number in the list that is repeated more often than any other	• Rewrite the numbers in order. • Determine the number that is repeated most frequently. • There can be more than one mode.	1, 2, 2, 2, (3, 3, 3, 3) 4, 4, 4

Visit ***go.SolutionTree.com/literacy*** *for a free reproducible version of this table.*

any rubric categories are weighted, input the score twice when calculating. Then translate the mode or median to a percentage using the scale at the bottom of figure 4.5, and assign a letter grade based on your school's percentage values for an A, A–, B+, and so forth.

Administering Preassessments

Preassessments are diagnostic and designed to ascertain what students know, understand, believe, or can do before approaching a lesson, unit, or course. In administering these, you collect data about students concerning particular skills and can use what you learn to inform your teaching practice (for example, you can determine whether to address individuals or arrange students into small groups to meet their needs by reteaching, extending, enriching, or modifying). Preassessments can uncover any misconceptions students have so that you can address them. Additionally, they can engage students in the upcoming work by piquing interest and priming them for the new material.

It is important to tell students that preassessments are not graded. The purpose is, instead, to collect information so that you can target your teaching more directly. In this way, preassessments are similar to formative assessments. Therefore, take notes or make a spreadsheet that identifies to what degree students perform in the various skill areas that the preassessment is meant to gauge. Your recordkeeping sheets can be as simple as a list of line items of each skill divided by categories. For example, the line items may include a grouping of grammar and convention skills—*format in-text citations, use active voice*—and a section for specific skills related to argument—*write a thesis to stake a claim, provide logical reasons, support reasons with evidence*. Next to each skill can be a simplistic indication of students' proficiencies, such as using a plus sign (*Got it!*), check mark (*Understood somewhat*), and minus symbol (*Not present or incorrect*). If desired, you can also log and record more comprehensive information to direct future planning. Review what you have recorded, and determine the next steps in your instruction.

Typically, preassessments are short and allotted minimal time to complete. However, in writing, asking students to respond to a prompt can help determine their writing strengths and weaknesses and whether they're aware of the elements and structure of a particular genre. You can also score preassessment writing samples on a rubric and examine more extensive data to guide instruction.

Here are some options for conducting writing preassessments. You might select and issue one or more for your writing unit.

- **Option 1: Use on-demand writing.** Achieve the Core (http://achievethecore.org) has on-demand writing prompts with complex text that students use as the basis for their responses. There are writing prompts for each of the text types—argumentation, informational/explanatory, and narrative—for grades K–5 and 6–12. You can use these on-demand writing prompts as preassessments and again as formative assessments at some point in your unit. (For links to these prompts, visit **go.SolutionTree.com/literacy**.)
- **Option 2: Review writing samples from a particular genre to identify purpose and characteristic elements.** Select and distribute an exemplary writing model paper to students. Ask them to read the paper individually and identify the purpose for writing, along with any elements they can name. You can leave this open ended or provide a list of elements. Visit appendix B or **go.SolutionTree.com/literacy** for links to writing sample resources.
- **Option 3: Compare and contrast writing samples.** Distribute a weak and a strong sample of a particular genre to students. Ask students to independently articulate in writing the differences between the two and justify their reasons for what contributes to the stronger piece of writing. Additionally, you can ask them to focus on and improve one aspect of the weak paper (for example, thesis or reason for an argument; setting or suspense for a narrative). Again, find appropriate student samples from appendix B provided in this text or the companion website, **go.SolutionTree.com/literacy**.
- **Option 4: Require open-ended responses.** Ask students to write responses to any of these: *Why do people write this kind of piece (or in this genre)? What are the elements of this particular genre? Can you create a graphic*

organizer to show the structure and relationship among these elements? Have you written in this genre before? If so, what was the topic? What might you have done to improve the paper you wrote, and what questions remain about this writing genre?

Summary

This chapter continues the backward planning approach by focusing on evidence of student learning, particularly curriculum-embedded performance assessments. Student writing checklists, presented early in the unit, along with the task, allow students to know the requirements of an assignment to maximize their chances of a successful product. The specificity of rubrics, including the scoring criteria, levels of performance, and criteria descriptors, contributes to their efficacy as an instructional tool to help students improve by self-assessing, critiquing peers' work, and understanding how you will grade their final papers.

Analytic rubrics are recommended for classroom use as students progress through the stages of the writing process so strengths and weaknesses can be pinpointed and this feedback can steer improvement. Holistic rubrics, although useful for school or district scoring, are more broad. Both the checklist and rubric are aligned to standards and KUDs and contain the genre-specific elements necessary to include in final written products to support students as they write.

Scoring student written work is subjective, which can pose problems when grading across a large group of students. However, scoring needs to be reliable and consistent, which rubrics can help achieve. Couple rubrics with consensus building—or calibration—in which teachers determine anchor papers that elucidate each performance level on a common rubric. This collaborative practice ensures that students across a school or district are afforded reliable and consistent scores. These anchor papers can be used to guide the scoring of students' papers and also during parent conferences. In teaching the many skills associated with writing, you should use these anchors as well as other student models and published work as instructional tools. When students have opportunities to examine and identify the strengths and weaknesses, they can determine what to emulate and what to avoid in their own work. You may like to supplement your unit design by administering preassessments. Preassessments are diagnostic tools to help identify students' previous knowledge or misconceptions so you can plan your unit to meet students' express needs.

The next chapter focuses on the last phase of backward design: designing differentiated lessons.

CHAPTER

5

Effective Lesson Design: The Gradual Release of Responsibility Model and Differentiation

Most of us have experienced the situation of teaching the same skill over and over without managing to produce the desired student results. We feel disappointed because we've let our students down. There could be numerous reasons for this frustration, but one could be not systematically and explicitly teaching the skill, strategy, or process in a way that yields success. That's where gradual release of responsibility can help—an instructional model for teaching new learning (Pearson & Gallagher, 1983). In this chapter, you will read about the aspects and benefits of this model along with a clear example, plus receive an inventory of generic ways and resources to differentiate instruction. When you create lessons for your unit, refer back to this text for support in finding appropriate lesson design and differentiation ideas.

The Gradual Release of Responsibility Model

The gradual release of responsibility model provides students with a continuum of support. It begins with teachers assuming control initially and moves to an eventual point where students take ownership of applying the new learning independently. David Pearson and Margaret Gallagher (1983) say this about the strategy:

> When the teacher is taking all or most of the responsibility for task completion, he is "modeling" or demonstrating the desired application of some strategy. When the student is taking all or most of that responsibility, she is "practicing" or "applying" that strategy. What comes in between these two extremes is the gradual release of responsibility from teacher to student. The hope in the model is that every student gets to the point where she is able to accept total responsibility for the task, including the responsibility for determining whether or not she is applying the strategy appropriately (i.e., self-monitoring). But the model assumes that she will need some guidance in reaching that stage of independence and that it is precisely the teacher's role to provide such guidance. (p. 35)

This model can be implemented when conducting a comprehensive lesson during one class period (for example, a fifty-minute or block schedule class) or during a series of lessons dedicated to more complicated learning topics. Inspired by Pearson and Gallagher (1983), Douglas Fisher and Nancy Frey (2014) divide the model into these four phases that together represent a fluid and cohesive instructional sequence.

1. Focused instruction ("I do it.")
2. Guided instruction ("We do it.")
3. Collaborative learning ("You do it together.")
4. Independent practice ("You do it alone.")

What follows is an explanation of what each component of gradual release of responsibility entails. In addition, I provide a specific example of how to conduct a lesson aligned to this model within a narrative writing unit centered on this guiding question: *How do I use descriptive details to develop a character?* You will notice while reading this sample lesson that it is a continuous string of lessons focused on using description to develop characters.

1: Focused Instruction—"I Do It"

Direct instruction is sometimes misunderstood because it conjures up an image of a teacher droning on in front of a classroom of listless and disinterested students. This is a false impression of what this type of teaching entails. Direct instruction is not didactic teaching, which is mostly associated with a teacher pontificating before disenfranchised students. Rather, it involves a series of orchestrated instructional moves that, when done well, can be highly successful in priming students to acquire new learning. Focused instruction involves the following aspects.

- Setting the purpose for learning
- Modeling or demonstrating student tasks and using think-alouds
- Inviting brief participation to check for understanding

Setting the Purpose for Learning

Allot a few minutes to set the stage for learning. Specifically state the purpose by posing and posting a guiding question appropriately written for the students. Or pique students' interest and then present the guiding question, as shown in the following lesson example.

> **Lesson example:** Feature a paragraph about a character in which the topic sentence reveals a personality trait, perhaps through implication, and the rest of the paragraph lacks supporting descriptive details about this character's personality. Ask students to turn and talk with a partner to share their observations of it. You might ask, "What do you know about this character?" Invite some students to share their thinking with the class. Once students draw the conclusion that it is weak on details to support the trait, reveal the guiding question to set the purpose for learning: "How do I use descriptive details, including figurative language, to develop a character?" Write this guiding question on a whiteboard or chart paper, and refer to it throughout the lesson.

Include a brief segue that helps students connect what they previously learned with the upcoming new information. Explain the importance of the lesson and what they will be expected to learn and accomplish at the conclusion of instruction. You might even consider other ways to draw students in, such as showing an intriguing object or picture, asking them to imagine an unusual situation, or featuring gibberish on the board that they can't help but try to decipher to illustrate a particular point (such as why grammar conventions assist readers).

> **Lesson cont'd:** You might say, "Let's revisit the paragraph that was void of details." (Reiterate their responses concerning its lack of details.) Continue with, "If writers don't vividly describe their characters, readers may not connect with them, understand their motives, or comprehend why others react to them the way they do. Readers might even be frustrated. Yesterday, we focused on personality traits in general and ones you might decide to use associated with the protagonist or antagonist for your stories. We also chose one trait and wrote a topic sentence for a character named Kimmie. Now we will zero in on writing a structured

paragraph with figurative language to give readers a clear description of this character. At the end of this lesson, you will have strategies and ideas for how to write descriptive details to develop a character's personality that you can apply to your own story."

Modeling Student Tasks and Using Think-Alouds

Input information so students have necessary content, model how to perform the task and what the end product will ultimately look like, and check for understanding to monitor progress so students proceed to the next step only when ready (Hattie, 2009). You may present information that facilitates learning through reading, listening, lecturing, discussing, discovering, observing, and so forth. When modeling—which occurs after, along with, and even before the information is presented—use the think-aloud strategy. In doing so, literally share out loud what you think so students can hear your thought processes and see you doing the work. Point out any potential stumbling blocks along the way that might impede accomplishing the task, and identify ways to address these issues to produce the intended outcomes. Additionally, explain what constitutes a quality end result or product using pertinent examples and showing what aspects make it so. If tools are needed, explain how to use them. Some such tools may include sample student writing, published text, graphic organizers, text features, or excerpts. If useful, provide a handout that aids students in accomplishing the task, and perhaps include helpful examples. (See chapter 4 for strategy suggestions and resource links for sample text and graphic organizers.)

Fisher and Frey (2014) provide a clear distinction between modeling and demonstrating:

> We think of *modeling* as an instructional move used when the lesson addresses using a cognitive process, such as reading, writing, mathematics, and such. *Demonstrating* is what a teacher does when focusing on physical tasks, such as the proper stance for swinging a baseball bat or the procedure for turning on a Bunsen burner. (p. 26)

Thus, our examples are forms of modeling since they rely on showing students how to write.

Lesson cont'd: Continue to compose a body paragraph on an electronic device or document camera that has the following topic sentence already written from an earlier exercise, perhaps the day before or even later on the same day. Talk aloud about what you are thinking as you write, and even stumble while doing so, correcting your work. Here is what you might say and write:

"Yesterday, I identified the character Kimmie and assigned this trait to her: popular. You helped me write this topic sentence using figurative language to vividly describe her personality without directly stating, 'She is popular.'"

> *Kimmie enters, causing a visible stir of excitement as eyes swivel in her direction, and people eagerly gravitate to her as if an imaginary string draws them within her sphere.*

"Now that I have a topic sentence, I need to add details to support it. Let's see. Who comes near her to show her popularity? Do a bunch of people surround her? Hmmm. I should start with one."

> *Yasmine comes over to her.*

"That's pretty weak."

> *Yasmine sidles up to her.*

"Better because I like the verb *sidles*."

> *Yasmine approaches, and others follow in her wake.*

"Maybe I'll just start with Yasmine and later write about others flocking to her to show her popularity."

> *Yasmine is the first to approach and sidles up to her like a beloved pet does her master.*

"I don't like that, as it appears that it's a hierarchy situation, which it's not. They're close friends and equals. Plus, it lacks description. Let me try again."

> *Yasmine sidles next to her on a vacant stool threadbare with overuse. Capturing Kimmie's attention, she chats enthusiastically about the dreadful Uber driver who took her out of the way before arriving at the restaurant.*
>
> "It's a good start, but I need more supporting details for the topic sentence to further indicate her popularity. I'll think about others who enter the scene."

Inviting Participation to Check for Understanding

Take time for students to process the lesson, and overtly check for understanding to solicit their input at strategic points. Since you are modeling and thinking aloud while doing so, you are checking to determine if students understand this preliminary part of the lesson. As you progress through the other components of gradual release of responsibility, there will be other opportunities to assess understanding more formally and gather additional data. At this point, you might monitor student learning to collect information by asking them to:

- Respond to a prompt with thumbs-up, thumbs-down, or a fist (to indicate that they're not sure); choral response; double-sided cards; prepared mini-signs on Popsicle sticks; or electronic devices
- Turn and talk with a partner in response to a question; solicit volunteers to share with the class
- Point to, highlight, or underline salient parts of a text, graphic, picture, or directions

Observe and listen to students to determine who has achieved an appropriate level of proficiency and can move to the next step or who is in need of additional support. Take note of future differentiation strategies to implement (see page 83).

> **Lesson cont'd:** Stop for students to turn and talk in response to these prompts pertaining to the writing you modeled: (1) What personality trait describes Kimmie? (2) What description and type of figurative language do I use in the topic sentence? (3) How does the sentence about Yasmine support the topic sentence? Is there descriptive language in this sentence?

During the "I do it" phase—setting the purpose for learning, modeling student tasks and using the think-aloud strategy, and inviting participation to check for understanding—the teacher assumes primary responsibility for guiding learning. As the lesson continues, students are given the tools to increasingly garner more ownership toward mastery of the target skills.

2: Guided Instruction—"We Do It"

At this juncture, students practice the new skill or strategy under the teacher's supervision and guidance in a different context than what was modeled so they can transfer the learning. Using the data you observed or collected during focused instruction and any pre-assessments, arrange students in a suitable grouping configuration—in pairs, in trios, or even individually—to work on an activity. You might even group students during the first stage so they segue smoothly into the work they will do now in guided practice.

Formative assessment is a hallmark of this stage and continues into collaborative group work. Even though students might be working with others, move throughout the classroom checking for understanding to assess individual progress of the new information. During guided instruction, notice that students will be at different places in their mastery of the skill or strategy. Continuously give immediate and specific guidance and feedback that help them acquire the new learning. Do so by questioning, prompting, and discussing to elicit information and encourage them to reach further in their learning.

Monitor learning and periodically take note of individual behavior and performance to determine gaps or misconceptions. Use what you observe and what students produce to inform and differentiate instruction so they progress on the right track. Make sure to redirect, remediate, or repeat instruction, as needed, to scaffold support to meet students' varying needs. When appropriate, provide enrichment for students ready for more challenge. This might mean regrouping students, arranging groups of varying sizes, or permitting students to work at different paces. For example, a student might begin working alone and then partner with another, or students in original groups may reconfigure to work in other groups. Additionally, encourage students to be monitors of their own learning so they are aware of what necessary steps they can take to reach desired goals.

Fisher and Frey (2014) address the differentiated nature of this phase:

> Guided instruction is not the same for every group, nor does it necessarily happen every day for every student. It's not likely that you will meet with every group on a daily basis, especially if you're teaching at the secondary level. Instead, you might meet with each group one to three times a week, depending on the length of the lessons. Some students need more guided instruction than others . . . [It] should not be reserved for students who are struggling; those who perform at grade level but could be performing higher, as well as students who are advanced and need to be challenged, also deserve this type of targeted instruction and benefit from it. (p. 40)

Lesson cont'd: Ask students to work individually or with a partner to write one or more detailed sentences that support the topic sentence about Kimmie. Again, refer to the guiding question by asking them, "How can you use descriptive details to develop this character?" Walk around the room listening to conversations, reading their sentences, and scaffolding instruction to differentiate learning in any of these ways, as appropriate.

- If the support is incorrect, ask, "Does that detail match the personality trait? Think about someone you know who is popular. What does someone do to show he or she is popular? Take some time to think about it."
- If the detail is weak, ask, "Is there a more specific example you can give to support the trait?"
- If the descriptive details are strong, but the student can go further, suggest, "I see you have included similes well. Is there an opportunity for creating a metaphor or using personification?"
- To make a connection and provide a different example, say, "Remember when we read the story about the character ______________________? What descriptive example did the author give to support her being (selfish, selfless, courageous, and so on)?"
- To remind students of the task, ask, "Let's revisit the guiding question." Point to it. "What is the specific personality trait we're focusing on for Kimmie? Can you talk to me about our task and what suggestions you have to describe this character?"
- To provide a template for a simile, try, *"Kimmie is as popular as ______________________. Kimmie's popularity is like ______________________."*
- To add sensory details, ask, "Are there words or phrases that appeal to sight, sound, taste, touch, or smell that you can associate with Kimmie's character?"

3: Collaborative Learning—"You Do It Together"

Fisher and Frey (2014) emphasize the power of students working collectively to discuss and sort out meaning as a vital vehicle for making sense of what they are learning:

> When done right, collaborative learning is a way for students to consolidate their thinking and understanding. Negotiating with peers, discussing ideas and information, and engaging in inquiry with others gives students the opportunity to use what they have learned during focused and guided instruction. (p. 7)

Working together gives students the opportunity to solve problems, seek validation and clarification, articulate their thoughts, and question each other to arrive at ways to apply the new learning. Fisher and Frey (2014) state that collaboration—unfortunately an overlooked part of a lesson sequence—should be embedded conscientiously into instruction. Examples for orchestrating collaboration include reciprocal teaching, jigsaw reading, Socratic circles, simulations, games, group discussion during literature circles, collaborative writing, or other activities geared to learning targeted skills. During this phase, continue to monitor learning by observing and assessing students while they work with one another to determine who is or is not prepared to move into independent practice. Conduct guided instruction, as needed, to reteach or reinforce learning for those who need additional support.

Wrap up this phase of the lesson to provide a sense of closure. Emphasize the target skills related to writing, reiterate the purpose of learning, and highlight parts of your writing or students' examples that satisfy the criteria. As Hattie (2012) notes, "Closure is used to . . . help organize student learning, to help to form a coherent picture, to consolidate, to eliminate confusion and frustration . . . and to reinforce the major points to be learned" (p. 205).

Invite students to ask questions and clarify their thinking, as needed, so they can approach independent practice—the next step—prepared to succeed. You might conduct yet another informal formative assessment, such as turn and talk, response cards, finger signals, think-pair-share, or a digital equivalent, to collect data that confirm whether students are ready to work on their own or if reteaching is warranted.

Lesson cont'd: Instruct students to write a body paragraph in pairs or trios about a character in a text you are reading in class or in a literature circle book. In this way, the exercise serves the dual purpose of checking for understanding about the text and for skills in using descriptive details to craft a paragraph highlighting a character's personality trait. Pose this task:

"We have practiced adding details to develop a character named Kimmie. After crafting a topic sentence that avoided explicitly stating her trait, we worked on providing descriptive details that made her very real to readers. Sometimes we used precise and vivid words to add description; others times we used forms of figurative language, such as simile or metaphor or sensory detail (imagery). Now you will work with classmates to develop a character you choose from a book you are reading. The author likely has provided some details, including figurative language, for your chosen character. Your job is to write a paragraph that the author might have written using what you know about the character and incorporating these details. When finished, you'll share your paragraphs with another group and discuss what part of your writing is most vivid and even suggest what can be added."

4: Independent Practice—"You Do It Alone"

At this point in the lesson, ask students to again apply what they have learned in a novel situation. This time, however, they demonstrate understanding independently and fully assume responsibility for the cognitive load they've acquired. Instructing students to use these new skills in a different situation will allow them to prove that they can transfer learning and truly show proficiency. For example, if they practice researching to find evidence for a particular topic, like gun control or animal testing, they then apply this skill of accumulating evidence for their own argument topics. If students exhibit difficulty applying the new learning, repeat certain phases of the instructional model accordingly.

Lesson cont'd: Students apply learning by drafting a descriptive paragraph for a selected character in the narrative they are writing. You might say this:

"Now you are ready to take charge of your own learning. We've practiced writing descriptively to develop a character, so determine which character—protagonist or antagonist—you will focus on first for your narrative and start drafting a paragraph once you determine the personality traits you want to convey. Remember that dynamic characters change throughout the story, so perhaps you draft more than one paragraph to depict this transformation. When finished, put your paragraphs in your working folders (or save them electronically) to revisit later. You'll eventually incorporate what you write into your full story draft."

Flexibility of the Gradual Release of Responsibility Model

Although each component of the gradual release of responsibility model is presented in a linear fashion, there is flexibility in execution. You can repeat one or more parts, omit others, and sometimes even rearrange them. For example, although this model is intended for teaching new material, you can use it to reinforce or review learning, in which case not all components will be necessary. Some students might require more guided practice, and you can embed repeated opportunities for practice throughout a lesson. These additional opportunities for repeated independent practice should occur as needed before a culminating assessment to demonstrate understanding of discrete skills that together form a more complete picture.

You might teach a string of lessons that employ the phases of the model in different ways. This can occur when you teach several related skills that are progressive stepping stones culminating in an end product. For instance, if the ultimate goal is to write a thesis statement, the required skills may be as follows: (1) state the purpose of thesis statements, (2) recognize thesis statements in published and student work, (3) identify patterns in statements to determine common attributes, (4) critique thesis statements, and (5) draft a thesis. Although these skills and lesson components are important, you may perhaps lengthen, abbreviate, or omit certain aspects of gradual release as you see fit, as long as students eventually consolidate what they have learned and apply it independently by writing a thesis statement for their own papers.

While students are learning something new, do not feel compelled to grade everything. As Carol Ann Tomlinson and Tonya R. Moon (2013) state:

> Learning challenging content—really learning it so that it makes sense, is useful, and is transferable—takes hard work and lots of practice. Along the way to this kind of deep learning, false starts, mistakes, and redirection will necessarily occur. Grading everything students do discourages the very kind of grappling that is fundamental to complex thought and genuine understanding. (p. 130)

As students progress through the components of the gradual release of responsibility or another direct instruction model, be careful to observe and check their progress. Provide constructive feedback instead of grading each practice piece they produce. The more appropriate situation for issuing grades is after students have completed summative work.

The Importance of Differentiating Instruction

Throughout instruction, take stock of how students are faring by checking for understandings at strategic points, as explained and illustrated in the previous discussion of gradual release of responsibility. You can differentiate the content, process, or product based on students' readiness levels, interests, or learning profiles. Additionally, you can differentiate the learning environment by taking into account the physical surroundings and the affective climate or tone of the classroom. Conducting preassessments and continually observing and collecting student work to determine student needs and then differentiating accordingly optimize student learning.

Content is what we want students to know, understand, and do (see chapter 3) based on the standards. Consider two ways to differentiate content. According to Tomlinson (2001), "First . . . we can adapt *what* we teach. Second, we can adapt or modify *how we give students access* to what we want them to learn" (p. 72). To adapt the *what*, provide students with various kinds of information on new and different topics. To modify the *how*, allow them to access this information online or in print; through an article, book, video, or audio recording; or in Braille or a large-print version of text. Another way to differentiate how students grapple with content is through grouping configurations, such as working individually, with partners, or in small groups, or even with adult assistance.

Whereas content is called the *input*, since students are filling their brains with information, the *process* is the sense-making piece. Unless a situation allows students to internalize, process, and make sense of the content, it won't stick. Process encompasses a series of learning experiences in which students work with the material they have been exposed to. These are the activities and formative assessments that represent a significant part of any unit. Examples of process include issuing, observing, and assessing performance on exit cards, journal prompts, debates, quizzes, games, or graphic organizers, any of which can be differentiated.

When students demonstrate their knowledge and understanding, they produce a *product* as evidence of learning. Whereas content is the input and process is the sense making, consider the product as the output. In the writing unit, the product is centered on the writing performance assessment and measured against a rubric (see chapter 4). As mentioned previously, present the criteria of the culminating product early in the unit so students are well aware of the expectations and can take conscientious incremental steps toward the overarching goal.

Provide differentiation opportunities around content, process, and product that appeal to students' readiness levels, preferred modes of learning, areas of interest, and learning environment in any of the ways presented in this chapter. In terms of readiness, students vary in their current level of skill, knowledge, and understanding for different reasons:

> Some students lack background knowledge because they might have moved schools and missed a segment of learning, have a language barrier, have been disengaged from school, or have struggled with a learning issue that precluded them from fully grasping the material at the pace of their grade-level peers. Conversely, some students might possess more readiness because they grasp knowledge quickly and retain it, are voracious readers of a particular subject, independently seek knowledge beyond the classroom expectations, or have adults in their lives who engage them outside of school in an area of interest. (Glass, 2012, p. 176)

As an example of differentiation according to readiness level, steer students toward resources for their essays that are accessible because of appropriately challenging readability levels. Also, institute flexible time frames for students to progress through each phase of the writing process since some require more or less time than others at various points. Another way to differentiate by readiness is to devise a system to check in with students periodically based on need. Ask how they are doing and make astute observations about their progress so they feel supported. Scaffold instruction for those needing additional assistance in grasping a skill. Additionally, break down the writing task into manageable chunks, and provide support in using time well.

When differentiating instruction based on a learning profile, consider the manner in which students learn and work. Common learning profiles include Howard Gardner's multiple intelligences (http://multipleintelligencesoasis.org), such as verbal-linguistic and logical-mathematical; Robert Sternberg's analytical, creative, and practical intelligences (www.education.com/reference/article/triarchic-theory-of-intelligence); and Rita Dunn and Kenneth Dunn's learning style dimensions, including the physiological, which accounts for auditory, visual, tactile, and kinesthetic modes (http://wps.prenhall.com/wps/media/objects/863/884633/Volume_medialib/dunn.pdf). But do not assume that students have just one or two ways in which they learn that are consistent in different content areas. For instance, a student might prefer to watch a video about cell division on Khan Academy (www.khanacademy.org) and read biographies in social studies to learn about historical figures. As Tomlinson and Moon (2013) state:

> The goal of learning-profile differentiation should be to create more ways for students to take in, engage with, explore, and demonstrate knowledge about content, and then to help students develop awareness of which approaches to learning work best for them under which circumstances, and to guide them to know when to change approaches for better learning outcomes (Tomlinson & Imbeau, 2013). Teachers and students need to understand that categorizing or pigeonholing people is to both misjudge and limit them. (p. 11)

Last, appealing to areas of interest means focusing on topics that students are curious or passionate about and planning accordingly. For example, you may let students choose a topic of interest for their arguments or select

Table 5.1: Ideas for Differentiating Instruction—Readiness

Content
• Provide resources and supplemental materials at varying levels of readability, such as the following. ◦ Textbooks ◦ Newspaper articles ◦ Magazine articles ◦ Short stories ◦ Novels (chapters) ◦ Diaries or historical journals ◦ Technical manuals ◦ Computer software ◦ Websites ◦ Speeches ◦ Documents ◦ Lab reports ◦ Science periodicals • Consider the amount of reading. • Adjust what material to teach students.
Process
• Provide word labels. • Provide vocabulary lists at varying levels of challenge for students to incorporate in their writing or speaking. • Modify or extend directions. • Partially complete a graphic organizer. • Assign appropriately challenging graphic organizers, templates, and frames. • Create an assignment using cloze procedure. • Create tiered assignments that vary by level of challenge. (As a management tip, use color-coding or symbols.) • Consider the amount of writing. • Allow extra time to complete assignments. • Consider pacing adjustments to eliminate instruction of skills and concepts that students have previously shown to have mastered. • Provide reference materials at varying levels of readiness (different kinds of thesauruses, online resources, and dictionaries). • Create or find games and appropriately assign them to individuals, pairs, or groups based on readiness. • Assign particular electronic tools and apps. • Assign jigsaw reading to groups based on readiness levels. • Assign students to specific learning centers. • Teach or reteach a skill, concept, or topic for selected students in need of honing targeted learning. • Enrich learning to higher achievers ready for more sophistication or extensions. • Issue multiple levels of questioning. • Assign homework at varying levels of difficulty. • Assign varied journal prompts according to readiness. • Preselect websites and assign to students as they investigate a research question. • Issue appropriately challenging sets of manipulatives and prompts. • Provide tiered RAFT assignments (role, audience, format, and topic).
Product
• Create tiered products that vary by level of challenge. • Create and issue RAFT products based on readiness. • Create rubrics for different levels of learners, while keeping in mind overall standards.

Visit ***go.SolutionTree.com/literacy*** *for a free reproducible version of this table.*

a book to read for literature circles. When conducting debates to practice finding evidence and ways to introduce counterarguments, choose controversial issues of interest to your class.

Tables 5.1–5.3 (pages 85–87) provide several differentiation ideas to incorporate into lessons. The tables depict ways to differentiate lessons according to student readiness (table 5.1), learning profile (table 5.2), and interest (table 5.3) and are divided into categories of content, process, and product. Feel free to incorporate your own ideas or modifications into your lesson plans.

To differentiate instruction, review various suggestions in chapter 2 for electronic tools or apps that fit students' unique characteristics since the same tools and apps may not be suitable for all students in your classroom.

Additional differentiation strategies include the following.

- **Adult assistance:** Work (or have another adult work) with students or small groups to provide further explanation, reteaching, or enrichment.

Table 5.2: Ideas for Differentiating Instruction—Learning Profile

Content
• Use gestures, facial expressions, and articulation when reading or orally presenting new information. • Show props, artifacts, visuals, or extra visuals to further help students comprehend text or information. • Invite students to choose to read text individually or with partners. • Allow students to access content in a way that addresses their learning styles, such as the following. ◦ Computer software ◦ Videos ◦ Audio ◦ Interviews ◦ Speeches ◦ Demonstrations ◦ Texts (textbooks, articles, or poems) ◦ PowerPoint presentations ◦ Artwork or photographs ◦ Graphic representations
Process
• Read directions aloud, play them on an electronic device, or provide them in writing. • Offer read-alouds or independent reading as an option, when appropriate. • Allow choice of graphic organizers. • Offer technology as an option when working on a project with peers (Google Docs or classroom blogs). • Allow students to type or handwrite their work. • Provide choice in how students learn new words or facts (flashcards, graphic organizers, and songs). • Be flexible about where students work in the classroom (in a chair, on the floor, at a table, or near the window). • Be flexible about how students work in the classroom (working with a partner or alone, using noise-canceling headphones, or standing at an upright desk). • Create or find different kinds of games and allow students to choose which to play. • Use a combination of tactile (for example, using hands to manipulate objects, dice, materials, or sentence strips) and kinesthetic (for example, using the physical body to create a human graphic organizer) activities, as well as the more common auditory and visual ones. • Create and issue a RAFT or other assignments during formative assessment with choices that appeal to multiple intelligences.
Product
• Allow students choice in how they demonstrate knowledge for a performance assessment, such as by writing an article or poem, performing a skit or interview, using multimedia (such as PowerPoint or iMovie), drawing, using music, and so on. • Create and issue RAFT products from which students choose.

*Visit **go.SolutionTree.com/literacy** for a free reproducible version of this table.*

Table 5.3: Ideas for Differentiating Instruction—Interest

Content
• Provide resources with various topic choices (for example, allow students to choose a topic that interests them—argumentation essay or research report topic, historical figure, complex text, and so forth). • Provide different reading genres (such as biography or autobiography) and media formats to learn about a topic. • Conduct literature or nonfiction circles. • Use student-generated questions in lecture and Socratic discussions.
Process
• Allow students to choose apps and online tools. • Conduct jigsaw activities based on topic of interest. • Allow students to choose or create interest centers. • Create or find games and appropriately assign them to individuals, pairs, or groups based on interest. • Assign varied journal prompts according to interest. • Preselect websites for students to choose from as they investigate a research question. • Create and issue sets of manipulatives and cubing prompts based on interest. • Allow students to choose subtopics within a greater unit. For example, in a unit on colonial life, allow students to choose an individual topic—clothing, art, or religion—as the focus for an activity; in mathematics, create a scale drawing of a self-selected object.
Product
• Work with students to devise an independent study that culminates in a product; provide criteria for quality of product and clear work expectations. • Assign students to collect a sampling of their best work in a portfolio. • Allow students to determine a community need and create (or participate in) a service-learning project. • Provide student choice in a topic of interest as the basis for a culminating project. • Allow students to select and respond to an essay question to demonstrate understanding.

Visit ***go.SolutionTree.com/literacy*** *for a free reproducible version of this table.*

- **Extra modeling:** Provide extra modeling before individual, pair, or small-group work.
- **Peer support:** Assign peers to help further explain a task or articulate it in a different way. Be mindful not to overuse peers as tutors, as these students need to continue on their own learning paths.
- **Flexible grouping:** Arrange students in groups based on a variety of factors (like purpose of task, topic, resources, projects, group goals, and student needs).
- **Preview:** Provide students with a glimpse of an assignment or activity before it is presented in class. To do so, send it home for parents or older siblings to review with the student in advance before teaching it to the whole class.
- **Language:** Provide instruction in a student's native language, or allow students to work with an adult who speaks the same language to clarify content, lead a text-based question discussion, or help summarize material.
- **Enrichment:** Provide opportunities for students to extend learning and explore a topic or concept with more depth and complexity.

In addition, you may consider the following resources.

- **CAST (www.cast.org/our-work/learning-tools.html):** CAST offers a set of principles for developing curriculum to provide everyone with equal opportunities to learn and provides many useful differentiation suggestions for incorporating contemporary tools into instruction to make learning more accessible to all students.

- **Free Technology Toolkit for Universal Design for Learning (UDL) in All Classrooms (http://udltechtoolkit.wikispaces.com):** This toolkit includes graphic organizers, literacy, study skills, collaboration, writing, and more resources.
- **CAST UDL Exchange (http://udlexchange.cast.org/home):** With this tool, teachers can peruse and build resources, lessons, and more.

Summary

With backward design, once you are clear about learning outcomes (KUDs), evidence of learning, and success criteria (rubrics and checklists), you are primed to design and deliver lessons. Gradual release of responsibility is a model for devising instructional experiences to teach new skills, strategies, or processes effectively to students. Although there is flexibility in the order and the amount of time and intensity devoted to each aspect, they are all critical components to include in a lesson plan when there is new learning to be absorbed.

Avoid excessive grading when students are learning something new since they are in practice mode and need time to cultivate and develop their knowledge and understanding. Use your professional expertise and the lesson's targeted learning goals to determine how to implement this model. Students should be gradually handed the reins to learn something new so they can independently apply it in novel situations.

Now that you have identified your standards and KUDs, established a culminating assessment, and designed effective lesson plans for your unit, it's time to launch your unit. The following chapter will discuss piloting your unit, using anchor papers, and reflecting on the unit's success with students.

CHAPTER

6

Launching the Unit

You have learned about the fundamentals of designing and redesigning writing units—the importance of writing and its different types, the six stages of the writing process, options for using digital environments, an effective approach to unit planning (backward design), KUDs, culminating assessments and criteria for success, preassessments, lesson design through the gradual release of responsibility model, and options for differentiation. Now you're ready to step into the spotlight and launch your unit. This chapter details how to accomplish the following aspects of unit development.

- Pilot the unit.
- Discuss student work.
- Reflect on lessons.

Piloting the Unit

Try as you might to plan for any scenario, there are unforeseen situations that you might encounter during unit implementation, such as unintentionally omitting certain skills that needed to be targeted, missing an opportunity to differentiate, wishing you had led a particular discussion that yielded critical thinking, or failing to present the criteria early enough in the unit. To circumvent any future issues, catalog any opportunities for revision in real time when teaching each lesson while they're fresh in your mind. Later, reflect on your impressions and revise your teaching so that the next time, instruction will occur more smoothly and yield even better results in student achievement. This ongoing self-assessment will put you in good stead when beginning subsequent steps. If colleagues are teaching the same unit, everyone should share his or her reflections. Set up a system for note taking that works well, whether it is on the hard copy of the unit, in a journal, on a note-taking app, or electronically (perhaps on a Google Doc).

The following types of general questions can help foster thinking about how the unit went and give some direction for note taking to guide revision. In addition, consider devising a questionnaire for students to give feedback. It could include their impressions of personal successes and challenges, learning as a result of particular lessons or the whole unit, suggestions for future instruction, and identification of lessons or activities that were and weren't helpful in moving their learning forward. Such a questionnaire provides input that you might not have necessarily asked about or observed in students during instruction.

Consider the following questions for assessing *checklists*, *rubrics*, and *tasks*.

- Were the expectations clear to students? Did they understand the assessment criteria? Did you present these expectations early enough in the unit?
- Did you use the checklist or rubric as an effective teaching tool?
- Did the performance task include the right level of challenge? Did it ask students to aptly demonstrate understanding of the topic? Was it designed to elicit the desired learning outcomes?
- Was the language in the performance task well written or confusing? How can you revise it?

- Did students have choice in topic selection to foster engagement?
- Would it be helpful to include a calendar or other organizational system for students to keep track of their work? Were the time frames clear? Were the due dates realistic, or did they need to be altered?
- What did you glean from scoring student work and formative assessments that indicates revision opportunities?

Consider the following questions for assessing *lessons*.

- Was there enough modeling and collaboration before students were asked to apply the skill independently?
- What worked particularly well and why? What was unsuccessful and why?
- Did you employ varied instructional strategies? Were your chosen strategies effective for teaching a skill, or would alternate ones have worked better for certain students?
- Were students consistently and actively engaged in learning?
- Were there classroom management issues that might be attributed to a faulty lesson or to execution? How would you revise the lesson to address this?
- Was the unit map complete, or did it miss targeting specific skills that should have been addressed?
- Did the unit map include the right guiding questions, or should you add, delete, or revise any?
- Did students know the purpose of their learning? Did you clearly articulate each task?
- Should you add lessons, or were some unnecessary? If so, which ones?
- Should you grant any lessons more time, or did any go on too long? Should you differentiate timing for individual students or groups?
- Was there enough opportunity for self-assessment?
- Were the lessons rigorous enough to challenge all students?
- Were there appropriate instructional supports for struggling learners? Were there enrichment opportunities for high achievers?
- Were the resources easily available and accessible to all students? Were there opportunities for more differentiation?

Consider the following questions for assessing *technology use*.

- Were the electronic tools or apps productive? Did they serve the intended purposes?
- Did you introduce the online tool or app appropriately and thoroughly in order for students to use it correctly?
- Were there technology glitches that could have been avoided? In what way?
- Did the technology enhance the writing process and final product or deter students in some way? How so?
- Was there a different tool you wished students had used? Which one? How can you plan for this in the future?

Discussing Student Work

Chapter 4 discussed the importance of identifying anchor papers for students to critique and utilize during the writing process. It also mentioned the importance of calibration sessions between colleagues to ensure anchor papers and subsequent scoring standards are consistent across classes, schools, and the district and to prepare for scoring your students' papers. After piloting a unit, reconvene as a group to discuss and compare how you scored student work. Teachers might differ in what scores they issue to aspects of the paper or the paper as a whole. It is imperative to collaborate as colleagues, and perhaps lead another calibration session, this time with your own students' work. Revisit the protocol in leading these sessions discussed in chapter 4. In pilot unit calibration sessions, you and your colleagues should discuss differences in your interpretations of particular criteria items that you might not have noticed before.

Critically discuss and examine the data from each of your classrooms, and take action accordingly. Since the performance assessment is not necessarily a summative assessment, pay attention to what you learn from the data. Examining the array of student work will yield insights about instructional decisions that may pertain not only to your class or individual students but also across grade levels. Thus, you may consider reconvening with colleagues to discuss your findings together. What you discover can center on these kinds of questions.

- Are there trends in strengths and weaknesses?
- What skills were not evident in student work that need attention?
- How can I design lessons next time to target these skills?
- When should I teach these lessons and in what context?

Reflecting on Lessons

During the teaching of a unit, there is a constant stream of reflection and revision. Armed with the notes you recorded about areas for improvement within each lesson and when scoring your students' work, reflect on your findings. You may do this either independently, if you are teaching this unit alone, or with colleagues. Plan for revisions you want to make next time you teach the unit. If you are working with others, divide up duties to share the job of improving the unit. For example, maybe teachers need to add a new lesson to address other skills, collect more resources to help students research particular topics, address technology glitches, abbreviate a lesson that went on unnecessarily long, change the rubric, or reword or rewrite a performance for clarity. When working in a team, expect discussion and brainstorming about how to approach issues.

While it is easy to identify areas that need improvement, it is not always easy to decide how to fix something that turned out to be ineffective. Working collaboratively can aid everyone in finding a better way to approach parts of the unit that need attention. Set dates for completing action items so that the unit will be ready for implementation by the next semester or school year. The following year (or semester) when you teach this unit, continue to take notes; however, there should be minimal revisions at this stage.

Ultimately, this reflection stage should give you time to review and analyze the quantitative and qualitative information you've collected while piloting. This careful data consideration will provide the direction for meaningful revision in curriculum and instruction and lead to best possible outcomes for the students in your charge.

Summary

When piloting the writing unit, plan to take notes along the way while teaching to determine what worked and what didn't. Collaborate with colleagues to share impressions and student work based on the pilot. Select new anchor papers if necessary. Arrive at a plan for revision using the notes you've taken during the reflection stage so that changes are targeted and serve to boost student achievement. Dedicate this time to review and analyze the quantitative and qualitative information you've collected while piloting, and then implement needed changes for meaningful revision in curriculum and instruction.

Epilogue

Curriculum design is hard work and takes time to do well. Whether you are revising an existing unit you, a colleague, or a publisher wrote, or you're creating your own, it requires dedication, creativity, and knowledge of myriad skills and content.

As you decided to embark on a comprehensive writing unit of instruction and read through this book to gain insights, you likely experienced a range of emotions. Sometimes you may have felt validated; other times, a task or information may have given you moments of confusion or self-doubt. Hopefully, you will have experienced excitement and eagerness to dive into unit planning. That's the passion you were meant to harness and unleash.

Take stock of your own professional growth based on what you've read in this text. No doubt you've progressed enormously as you've challenged yourself to strive for depth, rigor, and clarity in what you teach and how you'll teach it. So pause to focus on how far you've come from the beginning of the process to the end.

On your quest to best serve students in our schools, seek input from colleagues and capitalize on collective expertise, since joint thinking sometimes yields results not previously considered. Whether you work in a small school or district or a large one, initiate collaboration by setting up meetings, tapping into social media, or getting involved in digital communities. Consider taking an online class to learn from professors and colleagues alike. My hunch is that you will welcome the collegiality to learn from others face to face or virtually, and they will certainly appreciate the insights you have to offer.

As a lifelong learner, you have added an arsenal of new learning and adaptations to your existing inventory of knowledge and skills. Your students and colleagues are fortunate to have you among them seeking new ways to improve your talents and sharing what you've learned. Thank you for allowing me to participate in your journey.

Appendix A

List of Figures and Tables

Appendix B

Professional and Student Resources

A plethora of writing resources are available online and, of course, in print. Additionally, there are organizations and associations that support teachers and provide a wealth of resources to enhance curriculum and instruction. Peruse the following categories and the provided links for valuable teaching and learning resources. Visit **go.SolutionTree.com/literacy** to access these resources.

General Writing Resources

Some of the following are appropriate for students; others are for teachers to use. General resources for researching, citing, writing text types and genres, grammar and conventions, the writing process, and others include:

- **Duke (University) Thompson Writing Program** (http://twp.duke.edu/twp-writing-studio/resources)
- **Google differentiated search lessons** (www.google.com/insidesearch/searcheducation/lessons.html)
- **Purdue University Online Writing Lab** (http://owl.english.purdue.edu/owl/resource/659/1)
- **University of Washington Tacoma's Teaching and Learning Center** (www.tacoma.uw.edu/teaching-and-learning-center/writing-resources-0)
- **The Writing Center at UNC–Chapel Hill's "Evidence" handout** (http://writingcenter.unc.edu/handouts/evidence)

Complex Texts

Peruse any of the following publications to find text you might want to use to teach a particular writing skill by featuring published and student samples. Or use and recommend pertinent articles as the basis for students' research for a paper they are writing.

- **Ebooks:** Access these websites to find free ebooks to download. You might grab a text excerpt and use it as the basis for classroom discussion or individual annotation or to highlight a writer's style or target a skill.
  - Project Gutenberg (www.gutenberg.org)
  - Eastoftheweb (www.eastoftheweb.com/short-stories/indexframe.html)
  - The Literature Network (www.online-literature.com)

- ***Hippocampus* (www.hippocampusmagazine.com):** This monthly online publication has various texts, including memoirs, essays, interviews, and more.
- **Letters About Literature (www.read.gov/letters/contests/winners/2016/index.html):** This site features letters of winning contestants from students in grades 4–12 in which they write to an author (living or dead) about how literature (a book, poem, or speech) affected them personally.
- **The Moth (https://themoth.org/stories):** This site includes an extravaganza of storytelling accessible in different ways—*The Moth Radio Hour*, the weekly Moth podcast, and a library of stories going back to 1997.
- **The *New York Times*'s Learning Network (http://learning.blogs.nytimes.com/2015/08/26/announcing-our-2015-16-student-contest-calendar):** The products of thirteen- to nineteen-year-old contest winners are accessible on the same page as the listings of the available contests. Check out and use these samples of editorials, vocabulary videos, poetry, rap, editorial cartoons, summer reading (responses to what students found most interesting in the *New York Times*), and reviews (of books, video games, concerts, restaurants, art exhibits, and more).
- **ProCon (www.procon.org):** This independent, nonprofit public charity provides a multitude of sources for pro and con perspectives of controversial issues. The topics are categorized for easy navigation and access, such as by most popular, health and medicine, education, politics, science and technology, and so forth. All sources are cited, so students can appropriately give attribution.
- **River of Words (http://riverofwords.org/poetry/2010/index.html):** This site features winners of a poetry and art contest (five- to nineteen-year-olds) that focuses on the theme of watersheds.
- **Sarah Mook Poetry Contest (www.sarahmookpoetrycontest.com/contest_results_2016):** Winners of the poetry contest in grades K–12 are featured on this site.
- **Storycenter (www.storycenter.org):** This site includes a venue for listening to and sharing stories worldwide, including intergenerational ones of civil rights and first-person narratives of struggle, courage, and transformation. Users create and access stories via StoryWork, digital storytelling, and other forms of digital media production.
- ***The Sun* (http://thesunmagazine.org):** This monthly online magazine features personal essays, short stories, interviews, poetry, and photographs.
- **Teen Ink (www.teenink.com/Contests/Winners1516):** Read and use any of the writing from teenage contest winners of their magazine, including fiction, nonfiction, and poetry, plus topical writing products on community service, environment, and travel and culture. There are also art winners featured on the magazine's cover.

Consider any of these adult or student publications to determine how you might use them within instruction.

- ***Detroit Free Press*** (www.freep.com)
- ***Junior Scholastic*** (http://junior.scholastic.com)
- **The *Miami Herald*** (www.miamiherald.com)
- ***National Geographic Kids*** (http://kids.nationalgeographic.com/kids)
- **The *New York Times*** (www.nytimes.com)
- **The *New York Times Upfront Magazine*** (http://upfront.scholastic.com)
- ***Scholastic News*** (http://magazines.scholastic.com)
- ***Scholastic Scope*** (http://scope.scholastic.com)
- ***Scholastic SuperScience*** (http://superscience.scholastic.com)
- ***Slate*** (www.slate.com)

- *Time for Kids Almanac* (www.timeforkids.com/search/site/almanac)
- *USA Today* (www.usatoday.com)

Graphic Organizers

- **edHelper.com** (www.edhelper.com/teachers/graphic_organizers.htm)
- **Education Oasis** (http://educationoasis.com/curriculum/graphic_organizers.htm)
- **Freeology** (http://freeology.com/graphicorgs)
- **Houghton Mifflin Harcourt Education Place** (www.eduplace.com/graphicorganizer)
- **Teacher Files** (www.teacherfiles.com/resources_organizers.htm)
- **TeacherVision** (www.teachervision.com/graphic-organizers/printable/6293.html)

Assessment Tasks

The following resources help you create performance assessments.

- **Literacy Design Collaborative (LDC)'s "Task Template Collection 3.0": Templates for grades K–12** (https://ldc.org/resources#LDC-Task-Template-Collection-3.0)
- **LDC's "Literacy Context: Science/Writing Mode: Argumentation": Science argument prompts and student anchor papers with annotations for grades 6–8** (http://goo.gl/1Xaf42)
- **Performance Assessment Resource Bank's "Performance Tasks": K–12 performance tasks across content areas** (www.performanceassessmentresourcebank.org/bin/performance-tasks)
- **Stanford Center for Assessment, Learning, & Equity's "Performance Assessment Quality Criteria"** (https://d3gxp3iknbs7bs.cloudfront.net/attachments/f55e2536-b154-48cf-bcb8-eb3aa9202e66.pdf)

Student Writing Models

Writing samples can help clarify expectations for students. Access examples at:

- **Achieve the Core's "Student Writing Samples"** (http://achievethecore.org/category/330/student-writing-samples)
- **Brown's Student Learning Tools** (www.mesacc.edu/%7Epaoih30491/StudentLearningTools.html)
- **Common Core State Standards for English Language Arts and Literacy in History/Social Studies, Science, and Technical Subjects: Appendix C—Samples of Student Writing** (www.corestandards.org/assets/Appendix_C.pdf)
- **Holt, Rinehart and Winston's "Holt Online Essay Scoring—Writing Prompts"** (http://my.hrw.com/support/hos/host_models_list_Fall_2006.html#MSExpository)
- **Literacy Design Collaborative's "Student Work Samples"** (https://ldc.org/resources#Student-Work-Samples)
- **Oregon Department of Education's "Writing Scored Student Work—High School"** (www.ode.state.or.us/search/page/?=527)

- **Oregon State University: Writing 121's "Argument" sample essays and web resources** (http://goo.gl/i5DR0t)
- **Thoughtful Learning's "Student Models"** (https://k12.thoughtfullearning.com/resources/studentmodels)

Rubrics

Rubrics can help you assess impartially and clarify expectations for students. The State of Washington Office of Superintendent of Public Instruction rubric, for example, includes K–12 assessments with prompts and rubrics for civics, economics, geography, history, and international perspectives. Access it and other helpful rubrics that you can adapt based on the information in chapter 4 and the assignment you will issue.

- **"Chapter 1: What Are Rubrics and Why Are They Important?"** from Susan M. Brookhart's *How to Create and Use Rubrics for Formative Assessment and Grading* (www.ascd.org/publications/books/112001/chapters/What-Are-Rubrics-and-Why-Are-They-Important¢.aspx)
- **Education Northwest's 6+1 Trait Rubrics** (http://educationnorthwest.org/traits/traits-rubrics)
- **Edutopia's "Resources for Using Rubrics in the Middle Grades"** (www.edutopia.org/rubrics-middle-school-resources)
- **Kathy Schrock's Guide to Everything: "Assessment and Rubrics"** (www.schrockguide.net/assessment-and-rubrics.html)
- **Literacy Design Collaborative's "Student Work Rubrics"** (https://ldc.org/resources#Student-Work-Rubrics)
- **"Peer Assessment,"** K. J. Topping's article in *Theory Into Practice*, *48*(1), 20–27
- **RubiStar**, an online tool to help instructors create rubrics (http://rubistar.4teachers.org/index.php)
- **The University of Wisconsin–Stout's "Rubrics for Assessment"** (www.uwstout.edu/soe/profdev/rubrics.cfm#writing)
- **The State of Washington Office of Superintendent of Public Instruction's "OSPI-Developed Assessments for Social Studies"** (www.k12.wa.us/SocialStudies/Assessments/default.aspx)
- **"Using Rubrics to Promote Thinking and Learning,"** H. G. Andrade's article in *Educational Leadership*, *57*(5), 13–18

Peer Review Resources

Please use the following resources to guide you in teaching and implementing peer reviews of student work.

- **Calibrated Peer Review** (http://cpr.molsci.ucla.edu/cpr/cpr_info/index.asp)
- **Eli Review** (https://app.elireview.com)
- **Peerceptiv** (www.peerceptiv.com)
- **PeerMark** (https://guides.turnitin.com/01_Manuals_and_Guides/Student/Classic_Student_User_Manual/19_PeerMark)
- **"The Reliability and Validity of Peer Review of Writing in High School AP English Classes,"** C. Schunn, A. Godley, and S. DeMartino's article in *Journal of Adolescent and Adult Literacy*, *60*(1), 13–23 (http://onlinelibrary.wiley.com/doi/10.1002/jaal.525/full)

Scoring and Calibration

The following resources support calibrating to score student work.

- **Rhode Island Department of Education's "Writing Calibration Protocol"** (www.ride.ri.gov/portals/0/uploads/documents/common-core/ride_calibration_process.pdf)
- **Stanford Center for Assessment, Learning, and Equity's "Semi-Structured Calibration Activity"** (http://goo.gl/FqBgs1)

Unit and Lesson Examples

Although this book asks that you design or redesign your own unit, it is helpful to see others' examples. You can revise, personalize, and use what fits your students' needs. These units include a host of lessons, activities, assessments, resources, and more that you might embed in your own unit.

- **Achieve the Core (http://achievethecore.org/category/411/ela-literacy-lessons):** Peruse hundreds of teacher-developed K–12 standards-aligned lessons by navigating around this site starting with the provided link. Filter your search to find what you need.
- **EngageNY (www.engageny.org):** This site includes curriculum materials for grades pre-K–12 in both mathematics and ELA. The ELA modules, which address the Common Core ELA standards, provide eight weeks of instruction and include assessments. They focus on ELA standards but also include social studies and science content.
- **English Language Arts Guidebook Units (https://learnzillion.com/resources/81666-english-language-arts-guidebook-units):** The Louisiana Department of Education, in cooperation with LearnZillion, has created and made available ELA units that include daily lessons, assessments, texts, blank and completed handouts, and student writing samples. There is also a portal to purchase published books aligned to classroom texts. The units adhere to Louisiana's standards, which are based on the Common Core, but address a variety of subjects.
- **"Persuasion Across Time and Space: Analyzing and Producing Complex Texts"—from the Understanding Language Initiative (grades 6–8; http://goo.gl/0cEiMl):** This five-lesson unit moves students from an introduction to persuasion to analysis of rhetorical devices and lexical, grammatical, structural, and organizational choices.
- **"Persuasion Across Time and Space" from Understanding Language (grade 7; http://ell.stanford.edu/teaching_resources/ela):** The dual purpose of this unit is to develop students' ability to meet ELA standards and also promote English proficiency for English language learners. Developed around famous persuasive speeches, the unit supports students in reading a range of complex texts, plus writing and speaking for different audiences and purposes.
- **Project Exchange (grades 9–12; http://goo.gl/tvhG9Y):** This is designed for high school teachers to share curriculum, resources, and materials, and also to collaborate about best practices in project-based design and implementation with one another. The site is hosted by Envision Schools, a nonprofit charter organization.
- **Reading Like a Historian (grades 9–12; http://sheg.stanford.edu/rlh):** The curriculum on this site engages students in historical inquiry. Each lesson includes primary documents intended for differentiation purposes. This curriculum teaches students how to investigate historical questions by employing a host of reading strategies. Instead of memorizing historical facts, students evaluate the trustworthiness of multiple perspectives on historical issues. They learn to make historical claims backed by documentary evidence.

- **The *New York Times*'s Learning Network (http://learning.blogs.nytimes.com/2015/08/26/announcing-our-2015-16-student-contest-calendar):** This site offers a broad compilation of materials and resources for teaching and learning across content areas utilizing content from the *New York Times*, such as articles, photographs, podcasts, and graphics. It offers free lesson plans, quizzes, essay contests, vocabulary acquisition ideas, and more.

Essay Contests and Submissions

Be mindful to heed the contest deadline dates, submission guidelines (word count, formatting, and other information) for entries, and required fees (if any). Some are geared to students only; others are open to anyone, including you!

- **Hippocampus (www.hippocampusmagazine.com/submissions):** This online magazine accepts submissions for memoirs, personal essays, and flash creative nonfiction (or a work of creative nonfiction in an experimental format).
- **Letters About Literature (www.read.gov/letters):** This is a contest for students in grades 4–12 in which they are asked to read a book, poem, or speech and write to the author (living or dead) about how it affected them personally.
- **The *New York Times*'s Learning Network (http://learning.blogs.nytimes.com/2015/08/26/announcing-our-2015-16-student-contest-calendar):** All sorts of contests are available for thirteen- to nineteen-year-olds, such as for editorials, vocabulary videos, poetry, rap, summer reading (responses to what students found most interesting in the *New York Times*), editorial cartoons, and reviews (of books, video games, concerts, restaurants, art exhibits, and more).
- **River of Words (http://riverofwords.org/contest_rules.html):** This contest, for five- to nineteen-year-olds (excluding nineteen-year-old college students), is focused on the watershed theme. It's designed to help youth explore the natural and cultural history of their surroundings and express themselves through art or poetry. English, Spanish, and American Sign Language poems, as well as collaborative poems, will be accepted.
- **Sarah Mook Poetry Contest (www.sarahmookpoetrycontest.com/home):** This is a poetry contest for students in grades K–12.
- **Scholastic Art and Writing Awards (www.artandwriting.org/the-awards/categories):** Students in grades 7–12 can submit writing in all sorts of categories, such as critical essay, drama script, flash fiction, poetry, science fiction, and more. There are also entries for art categories, including ceramics, fashion, jewelry, painting, and other creative endeavors.
- ***The Sun* (http://thesunmagazine.org/about/submission_guidelines/readers_write):** This online magazine accepts submissions for essays, interviews, fiction, and poetry.
- **Teen Ink (www.teenink.com/Contests):** This site offers a host of contest opportunities, including cover art, fiction, nonfiction, and poetry. It also sponsors writing contests on topics such as environment (solutions and ideas about a problem facing the planet), educator of the year (an amazing teacher in your life), community service (how you make the world a better place), and more.
- **Winning Writers (https://winningwriters.com):** This clearinghouse site for writing contests and services provides links to the best literary contests along with their rules. By subscribing to the free email newsletter, you'll learn more about each contest, including which ones are suitable for writers at the beginning, intermediate, and advanced stages of their careers. Plus, it cautions writers about contests and services to avoid lest they be taken advantage of or scammed.

Organizations and Associations

Organizations and associations provide a wealth of resources to their members and also to the public. Review the following to determine which might provide you the most support in unit development to effectively serve your students.

- **International Literacy Association (www.literacyworldwide.org):** Originally the International Reading Association (IRA), the International Literacy Association (ILA) has worked for the past sixty years to enhance literacy instruction through research and professional development. This membership organization is involved in a host of literacy efforts that include research journals, publications, professional development, conferences, and advocacy efforts. It also offers annual annotated reading lists of recently published books that children, young adults, teachers, and librarians select as their favorites. Access "Choices" reading lists at www.literacyworldwide.org/get-resources/reading-lists.
- **National Council of Teachers of English (www.ncte.org):** This professional association, which has been in existence for more than one hundred years, is composed of educators in English studies, literacy, and language arts. To support its membership, NCTE provides professional learning, programs, interest groups, publications, resources, research support, and projects.
- **ReadWriteThink (www.readwritethink.org):** This site, which is partnered with ILA and NCTE, provides free standards-aligned resources and materials for reading and language arts instruction to parents, educators, and other professionals.
- **National Writing Project (www.nwp.org):** NWP provides professional development, develops resources, generates research, and acts on knowledge to improve writing curriculum and instruction. It has a variety of sites and serves teachers across content areas from early childhood through the university level.
- **Stanford Center for Assessment, Learning, & Equity (http://scale.stanford.edu):** SCALE creates and develops performance assessments and solutions for states, districts, and educational foundations. It serves students and teachers from early childhood through college and career.

References and Resources

Atwell, N. (2015). *In the middle: A lifetime of learning about writing, reading, and adolescents* (3rd ed.). Portsmouth, NH: Heinemann.

Black, P., & Wiliam, D. (1998). Assessment and classroom learning. *Assessment in Education, 5*(1), 7–74.

Brookhart, S. M. (2013). *How to create and use rubrics for formative assessment and grading.* Alexandria, VA: Association for Supervision and Curriculum Development.

Bruner, J. S., Goodnow, J. J., & Austin, G. A. (1956). *A study of thinking.* New York: Wiley.

California Department of Education. (1998, October). *History–social science content standards for California Public Schools: Kindergarten through grade twelve.* Sacramento, CA: Author. Accessed at www.cde.ca.gov/be/st/ss/documents/histsocscistnd.pdf on July 1, 2016.

California Department of Education. (2005, January). *Physical education model content standards for California Public Schools: Kindergarten through grade twelve.* Sacramento, CA: Author. Accessed at www.cde.ca.gov/be/st/ss/documents/pestandards.pdf on July 1, 2016.

Carlson, R. (2000). *A don't sweat the small stuff treasury: A special collection for new parents.* New York: Hyperion.

Casner-Lotto, J., & Barrington, L. (2006). *Are they really ready to work?: Employers' perspectives on the basic knowledge and applied skills of new entrants to the 21st century U.S. workforce.* New York: The Conference Board, the Partnership for 21st Century Skills, Corporate Voices for Working Families, and the Society for Human Resource Management. Accessed at www.p21.org/storage/documents/FINAL_REPORT_PDF09-29-06.pdf on September 1, 2016.

Children's Online Privacy Protection Act of 1998, 15 U.S.C. 6501–6505 (1998).

Coleman, D., & Pimentel, S. (2012). *Revised publisher's criteria for the Common Core State Standards in English language arts and literacy, grades 3–12.* Accessed at www.corestandards.org/assets/Publishers_Criteria_for_3-12.pdf on May 3, 2016.

Council of Writing Program Administrators, National Council of Teachers of English, & National Writing Project. (2001, January). *Framework for success in postsecondary writing.* Accessed at http://wpacouncil.org/files/framework-for-success-postsecondary-writing.pdf on May 3, 2016.

Duke, N. K., & Pearson, P. D. (2002). Effective practices for developing reading comprehension. In A. E. Farstrup & S. J. Samuels (Eds.), *What research has to say about reading instruction* (3rd ed., pp. 205–242). Newark, DE: International Reading Association.

Duke, N. K., Pearson, P. D., Strachan, S. L., & Billman, A. K. (2011). Essential elements of fostering and teaching reading comprehension. In S. J. Samuels & A. E. Farstrup (Eds.), *What research has to say about reading instruction* (4th ed., pp. 51–93). Newark, DE: International Reading Association.

Emig, J. (1977). Writing as a mode of learning. *College Composition and Communication, 28*(2), 122–128.

Erickson, H. L. (2002). *Concept-based curriculum and instruction: Teaching beyond the facts.* Thousand Oaks, CA: Corwin Press.

Erickson, H. L. (2007). *Concept-based curriculum and instruction for the thinking classroom.* Thousand Oaks, CA: Corwin Press.

Fisher, D., & Frey, N. (2014). *Better learning through structured teaching: A framework for the gradual release of responsibility* (2nd ed.). Alexandria, VA: Association for Supervision and Curriculum Development.

Fitzgerald, J., & Shanahan, T. (2000). Reading and writing relations and their development. *Educational Psychologist, 35*(1), 39–50.

Fountas, I. C., & Pinnell, G. S. (2001). *Guiding readers and writers (grades 3–6): Teaching, comprehension, genre, and content literacy.* Portsmouth, NH: Heinemann.

Galdon, P. (1985). *The little red hen.* New York: HMH Books for Young Readers.

Glass, K. T. (2012). *Mapping comprehensive units to the ELA Common Core standards, K–5.* Thousand Oaks, CA: Corwin Press.

Glass, K. T. (2013). *Mapping comprehensive units to the ELA Common Core standards, 6–12.* Thousand Oaks, CA: Corwin Press.

Graff, G., & Birkenstein, C. (2014). *"They say / I say": The moves that matter in academic writing* (3rd ed.). New York: Norton.

Graham, S., & Hebert, M. A. (2010). *Writing to read: Evidence for how writing can improve reading—A Carnegie Corporation Time to Act report.* Washington, DC: Alliance for Excellent Education.

Graham, S., & Perin, D. (2007). *Writing next: Effective strategies to improve writing of adolescents in middle and high schools—A report to Carnegie Corporation of New York.* Washington, DC: Alliance for Excellent Education.

Hattie, J. (2009). *Visible learning: A synthesis of over 800 meta-analyses relating to achievement.* New York: Routledge.

Hattie, J. (2012). *Visible learning for teachers: Maximizing impact on learning.* New York: Routledge.

Hattie, J., & Yates, G. (2014). *Visible learning and the science of how we learn.* New York: Routledge.

Hess, K. K., Jones, B. S., Carlock, D., & Walkup, J. R. (2009, March 7). *Cognitive rigor: Blending the strengths of Bloom's taxonomy and Webb's Depth of Knowledge to enhance classroom-level processes.* Accessed at http://files.eric.ed.gov/fulltext/ED517804.pdf on September 1, 2016.

Kadushin, A., & Harkness, D. (2002). *Supervision in social work* (4th ed.). New York: Columbia University Press.

Kilgore, N. (2012, January 25). *How to host a book club.* Accessed at http://lifestyle.howstuffworks.com/event-planning/how-to-host/how-to-host-book-club1.htm on May 5, 2015.

Kittle, P. (2008). *Write beside them: Risk, voice, and clarity in high school writing.* Portsmouth, NH: Heinemann.

Kohn, A. (2006). *The homework myth: Why our kids get too much of a bad thing.* Cambridge, MA: Da Capo Press.

Literacy Design Collaborative. (2014). *LDC task template collection version 3.0.* Accessed at https://ldc.org/sites/default/files/ldc-resource-library-files/LDC%20Task%20Template%20Collection%20Version%203.0.pdf on September 1, 2016.

Mantsios, G. (1992). Rewards and opportunities: The politics and economics of class in the U.S. In P. S. Rothenberg (Ed.), *Race, class, and gender in the United States: An integrated study* (2nd ed., pp. 96–110). New York: St. Martin's Press.

Middlebury Interactive Languages. (n.d.). *A tapestry of language: A look at languages spoken by ELLs across the U.S.* Accessed at www.middleburyinteractive.com/sites/default/files/MIL-ELL-Infographic-072915.pdf on May 5, 2016.

National Commission on Writing in America's Schools and Colleges. (2003, April). *The neglected "R": The need for a writing revolution.* New York: College Entrance Examination Board.

National Commission on Writing for America's Families, Schools, and Colleges. (2004, September). *Writing: A ticket to work . . . or a ticket out—A survey of business leaders.* New York: College Entrance Examination Board.

National Commission on Writing for America's Families, Schools, and Colleges. (2005, July). *Writing: A powerful message from state government.* New York: College Entrance Examination Board. Accessed at www.collegeboard.com/prod_downloads/writingcom/powerful-message-from-state.pdf on May 4, 2016.

National Governors Association Center for Best Practices & Council of Chief State School Officers. (n.d.a). *Common Core State Standards for English language arts and literacy in history/social studies, science, and technical subjects: Appendix A—Research supporting key elements of the standards.* Washington, DC: Authors. Accessed at www.corestandards.org/assets/Appendix_A.pdf on May 4, 2016.

National Governors Association Center for Best Practices & Council of Chief State School Officers. (n.d.b). *Common Core State Standards for English language arts and literacy in history/social studies, science, and technical subjects: Appendix B—Text exemplars and sample performance tasks.* Washington, DC: Authors. Accessed at www.corestandards.org/assets/Appendix_B.pdf on May 4, 2016.

National Governors Association Center for Best Practices & Council of Chief State School Officers. (n.d.c). *Common Core State Standards for English language arts and literacy in history/social studies, science, and technical subjects: Appendix C—Samples of student writing.* Washington, DC: Authors. Accessed at www.corestandards.org/assets/Appendix_C.pdf on May 4, 2016.

National Governors Association Center for Best Practices & Council of Chief State School Officers. (2010). *Common Core State Standards for English language arts and literacy in history/social studies, science, and technical subjects.* Washington, DC: Authors. Accessed at www.corestandards.org/assets/CCSSI_ELA%20Standards.pdf on May 4, 2016.

Olds, S. (1982, August 2). Liddy's oranges [Poem]. *The New Yorker*, 79.

Ontario Ministry of Education. (2006). *The Ontario curriculum (grades 1–8): Language.* Toronto: Author. Accessed at www.edu.gov.on.ca/eng/curriculum/elementary/language18currb.pdf on May 3, 2016.

Owen, D. (2015). Beyond taste buds: The science of delicious. *National Geographic.* Accessed at http://ngm.nationalgeographic.com/2015/12/food-science-of-taste-text on May 5, 2015.

Pearson, P. D., & Gallagher, M. C. (1983, October). *The instruction of reading comprehension* (Technical Report No. 297). Champaign, IL: Center for the Study of Reading, University of Illinois at Urbana–Champaign.

Popham, W. J. (2008). *Transformative assessment.* Alexandria, VA: Association for Supervision and Curriculum Development.

Pritchard, R. J., & Honeycutt, R. L. (2006). The process approach to writing instruction: Examining its effectiveness. In C. A. MacArthur, S. Graham, & J. Fitzgerald (Eds.), *The handbook of writing research* (pp. 275–290). New York: Guilford Press.

Reeves, D. (2016). *FAST grading: A guide to implementing best practices.* Bloomington, IN: Solution Tree Press.

Rhode Island Department of Education. (2013). *Writing calibration protocol.* Accessed at www.ride.ri.gov/Portals/0/Uploads/Documents/Common-Core/RIDE_Calibration_Process.pdf on May 6, 2016.

Rogers, P. (2014, November 17). Massive starfish die-off in Pacific Ocean linked to mystery virus. *Mercury News.* Accessed at www.mercurynews.com/news/ci_26954958/massive-starfish-dieoff-in-pacific-ocean-linked-to-mystery-virus on May 5, 2016.

Rohman, D. G. (1965). Pre-writing: The stage of discovery in the writing process. *College Composition and Communication, 16*(2), 106–112.

Shanahan, T. (2006). Relations among oral language, reading, and writing development. In C. A. MacArthur, S. Graham, & J. Fitzgerald (Eds.), *Handbook of writing research* (pp. 171–183). New York: Guilford Press.

Silverstein, S. (n.d.). *Dirty face* [Poem]. Accessed at www.familyfriendpoems.com/poem/dirty-face-by-shel-silverstein on May 5, 2015.

Spandel, V. (2001). *Creating writers: Through 6-trait writing assessment and instruction* (3rd ed.). New York: Longman.

Spandel, V. (2013). *Creating writers: 6 traits, process, workshop, and literature* (6th ed.). Boston: Allyn & Bacon.

Stanford Center for Assessment, Learning, and Equity. (n.d.). *Semi-structured calibration activity*. Accessed at http://performanceassessmentresourcebank.org/system/files/SCALE%20Semi-Structured%20Calibration%20Activity%20Protocol.pdf on May 5, 2016.

Stanford Center for Assessment, Learning, and Equity. (2015). *Designing for deeper learning: How to develop performance tasks (Fall-15)* [Interview transcript]. Accessed at http://online.stanford.edu/courses on September 7, 2015.

Texas Education Agency. (2015). *19 TAC chapter 110. Texas essential knowledge and skills for English language arts and reading*. Accessed at http://ritter.tea.state.tx.us/rules/tac/chapter110/index.html on May 3, 2016.

Tierney, R. J., & Shanahan, T. (1991). Research on the reading-writing relationship: Interactions, transactions, and outcomes. In R. Barr, M. L. Kamil, P. Mosenthal, & P. D. Pearson (Eds.), *Handbook of reading research* (Vol. 2, pp. 246–280). Mahwah, NJ: Erlbaum.

Tomlinson, C. A. (2001). *How to differentiate instruction in mixed-ability classrooms* (2nd ed.). Alexandria, VA: Association for Supervision and Curriculum Development.

Tomlinson, C. A., & Imbeau, M. B. (2013). Differentiated instruction: An integration of theory and practice. In B. J. Irby, G. Brown, R. Lara-Alecio, & S. Jackson (Eds.), *The handbook of educational theories* (pp. 1081–1101). Charlotte, NC: Information Age.

Tomlinson, C. A., & Moon, T. R. (2013). *Assessment and student success in a differentiated classroom*. Alexandria, VA: Association for Supervision and Curriculum Development.

Virginia Department of Education. (2010). *English standards of learning for Virginia Public Schools: Grade 7*. Accessed at www.doe.virginia.gov/testing/sol/standards_docs/english/2010/stds_english7.pdf on May 4, 2016.

Walqui, A., Koelsch, N., & Schmida, M. (n.d.). *Persuasion across time and space: Analyzing and producing complex texts—A unit developed for the Understanding Language Initiative by WestEd's Teacher Professional Development Program*. Stanford, CA: Understanding Language, Stanford Graduate School of Education. Accessed at http://ell.stanford.edu/sites/default/files/ela_pdf/ELA%20Unit%20Introduction_0.pdf on May 5, 2016.

White, P. (2014). Learning the languages of appreciation. *Educational Leadership*, *71*(5), 30–34.

Wiggins, G. (2012). Seven keys to effective feedback. *Educational Leadership*, 70(1), 10–16. Accessed at www.ascd.org/publications/educational-leadership/sept12/vol70/num01/Seven-Keys-to-Effective-Feedback.aspx on September 2, 2016.

Wiggins, G., & McTighe, J. (1998). *Understanding by design*. Alexandria, VA: Association for Supervision and Curriculum Development.

WikiHow. (n.d.). *Hand washing clothes*. Accessed at www.wikihow.com/Wash-Your-Clothes#Hand_Washing_Clothes_sub on September 21, 2016.

Witte, S. (2013). Preaching what we practice: A study of revision. *Journal of Curriculum and Instruction*, *6*(2), 33–59. Accessed at www.nwp.org/cs/public/download/nwp_file/17665/witte_preaching_what_we_practice.pdf?x-r=pcfile_d on May 3, 2016.

Zarefsky, D. (2005). *Argumentation: The study of effective reasoning* (2nd ed.). Chantilly, VA: Teaching.

Index

D

E

F

G

H

I

S

T

U

V

W

Y

(Re)designing Argumentation Writing Units for Grades 5–12
Kathy Tuchman Glass
Developed for teachers, curriculum designers, and literacy coaches, this user-friendly guide offers practical recommendations, strategies, and tips for establishing argumentation units of instruction that empower students to artfully and logically present and convince others of their position.
BKF708

Using Technology to Enhance Writing
Edited by Richard E. Ferdig, Timothy V. Rasinski, and Kristine E. Pytash
Sharpen your students' communication skills while integrating digital tools into writing instruction. Loaded with techniques for planning and organizing writing, this handbook troubleshoots issues students face when writing in a printed versus digital context and teaches them how to read in multiple media.
BKF607

What Principals Need to Know About Teaching and Learning Writing
Ruth Culham
Discover practical strategies for supporting and assessing writing instruction in all content areas while equipping teachers with instructional practices that emphasize this critical skill, which students need to adapt to the demands of the CCSS and thrive in the 21st century.
BKF557

Instructional Planning for Effective Teaching
James H. Stronge and Xianxuan Xu
Explore research-based instructional planning tools teachers, leaders, and administrators can use in everyday practice. Discover powerful strategies and guidelines for developing quality lessons, setting learning objectives, planning differentiated instruction, and designing technology-integrated learning to effectively teach and challenge every student.
BKF642

Teaching Common Core English Language Arts Standards
Patricia M. Cunningham and James W. Cunningham
Explore twenty lesson frameworks to help teach the Common Core State Standards for English language arts. Discover targeted lessons to help students master critical skills, including how to organize ideas from informational texts, identify similarities and differences, and write with grade-appropriate language.
BKF617